HOW TO

Study

HOW TO
Study

The Comprehensive Guide
For
Students Of All Ages

By Ronald W. Fry

THE CAREER PRESS
P. O. Box 34
Hawthorne, NJ 07507
1-800-CAREER-1

HOW TO STUDY: The Comprehensive Guide for Students of All Ages, ISBN 0-934829-54-3, $10.95.

Copies of this volume may be ordered by mail or phone directly from the publisher. To order by mail, please include price as noted above plus $1.00 shipping and handling for each book ordered. Send to: The Career Press Inc., 62 Beverly Rd., PO Box 34, Hawthorne, NJ 07507

Or call Toll-Free 1-800-CAREER-1) to order using your VISA or Mastercard or for further information on all books published or distributed by The Career Press.

90-0782WAR

TABLE OF CONTENTS

HOW TO

Study

HOW TO
Use
This
Book

INTRODUCTION

> What one knows is, in youth, of little moment; they
> know enough who know how to learn.
> — Henry Adams

How to *study?* What's the big deal? You're no brain, but you've got a C average. Besides, you don't have *time* to do more —football practice starts Monday. And why would you want to waste your time reading a book about something you don't want to do in the first place?

Believe it or not, there are some terrific answers to those questions. But before I start convincing you why learning proper study skills really *is* important, let's figure out what we mean by "study skills" so we're on the same wavelength.

Yes, **How To Study** includes hints, advice and techniques for taking notes in class, while you're reading your textbooks, even in the library. And how to prepare for tests. And how to organize your study schedule to get the best results in the shortest amount of time. But that's the *last* half of the book. There are essential skills you may think have nothing to do with studying, important steps you need to take right now.

OK, Where Do I Start?

Learn as though you would never be able to master it;
hold it as if you would be in fear of losing it.
— Confucius

Developing great study habits is like a race between you
and all your friends around a track. Before you can declare a
winner, you have to agree on where the finish line is. In other
words, how do you measure your ability to use these skills?
What's good? What's poor?

But you can't even start the race until you know where
the *starting* line is...especially if everybody is starting from a
different place on the track!

Chapter 1 starts by explaining each study skill and clar-
ifying how each can and should function in your life. Then I
give you a chance to find your own starting line.

This first chapter is the most important in **How To
Study**, because your own honest assessment of how well you
have already mastered basic study habits will set the tone for
your entire approach to the guidelines you will find throughout
this book.

In Chapter 2, you'll learn the importance of where, how
and when you study and start building the study environment
that's perfectly right for *you*. Why is this important? If you've
spent three hours reading <u>Moby Dick</u> with Poison shaking the
walls, it's not surprising that you're still on shore. Reading
and understanding Mr. Melville might have little to do with
increasing your reading comprehension, rescheduling your
time or changing books and a lot more to do with just turning
down the radio. (Alternatively, those of you who have trouble
studying in a hush-hush library might find a Walkman actually helps you concentrate!)

There is no magic elixir in the study habit regimen. If math and science are not your strong suits, scanning **How To Study** will not transform you into a Nobel Prize-winning physicist. Nobody is great at *every*thing, but everybody is great at *some*thing.So you'll also get a chance to rate the subjects you like and dislike, plus those classes you do best and worst in. You'll find in later chapters that applying yourself to the subjects in which you need the most work is a simple, logical and successful way to alter your current habits without necessarily studying harder or longer.

Chapter 2 also introduces some of the "intangibles" in the study equation: your home environment, attitude, motivation, etc. If you are dedicated to the study discipline and motivated to achieve certain goals, all the other factors that affect your study habits will fall more naturally into place. A belief in the study ethic is one of the keys to success.

Reading & Remembering

Chapter 3 introduces the two skills basic to any study process: reading and memorization. No matter how well you learn to take notes, how familiar you become with your library, how doggedly you study for tests, if you are reading wrong (or not enough) and not remembering what you read, life will be difficult.

Becoming a reader is a skill, one usually acquired early in life. If it's a skill you haven't acquired yet, now is the time!

Effective reading is a combination of speed, comprehension and retention. Chapter 3 will help you find the proper balance of these three elements. It will also help you work on concentration—the ability to focus on the printed page to the exclusion of all else—a skill that all superior readers have.

Learning how to remember more of what you read is just as important as reading faster. Chapter 3 also points out how your ability to recall ideas, facts and figures can be significantly increased (both quantitatively and qualitatively) with the right kind of practice.

"If I Only Had More Time!"

To see a significant change in your life, many of you will not need to study *more,* just *smarter.* Which means making better use of your study time. Chapter 4 introduces organizational and time management tools you can use to make sure you are always on track, including guidelines to develop both a short-term assignments calendar and long-term project and test scheduling calendar.

Go To The Head Of The Class

In chapter 5, I talk about the one experience we all have in common, no matter how old we are—the classroom. I'll help you take better notes, encourage your active participation in class discussions—including pointers on how to overcome the more natural tendency to hide behind the potted plant in the back of the room—and get more out of lectures.

Learning Your Library

Chapter 6 introduces you to the single most important resource in your study career—your library. Whether you live in a small town, where library volumes are counted in the thousands and "current" might mean five years old, or a large city, where the library stacks kiss the sky and contain answers you don't even have questions for yet, learning how to take advantage of this great collection of knowledge is very important. You'll learn about the kinds of books, periodicals, newspapers, magazines, computer software, video and audio tapes and other reference materials available to you and suggestions for how to find and use them, including an explanation of the Dewey Decimal Classification System.

Move Over Mr. Dickens

No matter how confident you are in your writing ability, I doubt you cheer when papers are assigned. Get used to it. By the time you get to college, term papers will be a regular part of virtually every class you take. And don't think graduation ends the chore. You'll be writing "papers" of some kind—business letters, presentations, proposals, long memos—in almost any career you choose. And your ability to clearly and concisely express your views and communicate facts, figures and ideas may well strongly influence how fast you advance in your chosen career.

I'm convinced that too many of you place the emphasis in "writing papers" on the word "writing." By introducing you to a remarkably easy way to take notes for papers and helping you break down any paper, no matter how complex, into twelve easy-to-follow steps, I think you'll find you create papers infinitely better than before...even if you're still no threat to Mr. Dickens when it comes to writing.

Use A No. 2 Pencil

Chapter 8 covers the do's and don'ts of test preparation, including the differences between studying for weekly quizzes, midterms and final examinations, why last minute cramming doesn't work, studying for and taking different types of tests (multiple choice, essay, etc.), how to increase your guessing scores, even which questions to answer first and which to leave for last.

That's Nice. So What?

Nobody gives a hoot about what I did at (the University of) Michigan. I will be judged on this opportunity, on this level."

— Jim Harbaugh, Chicago Bears

Now that you know what you're going to learn from this book, why bother going through the whole thing?

Well, the answer sounds like one of those "'Why?' 'Because'" scenes your parents put you through: Whether you *want* to or not, whether you *like* to or not, you do *have* to study. For better grades? To get into a better college? Succeed in school? Keep your parents off your back?

In part, but not really: ***Learn to study to succeed in LIFE.*** Sooner or later, you *will* be out of school. But you will *never not* have to study. So you might as well get the habit early.

Whether you want to be an engineer, doctor, construction worker, artist, dancer, auto mechanic or businessman, be prepared to study. Never have the demands of our society been so great and the burdens on individuals so great.

As Jim Harbaugh so eloquently expressed it, what you know *now* and can do *now* is all anyone else cares about. How important is *his* past—high school football star, college football star, All-American, top NFL draft choice? Nice, but no cigar. He's now a third-string quarterback on a professional football team. He has to know and be able to execute, without a moment's hesitation, hundreds of different plays with thousands

14

of variations. If he does, the bonuses for reaching the Super Bowl—getting an "A" in his life—are substantial. If he does not, large people with no necks will show him the error of his ways in a most unpleasant fashion. He has to study now, learn now, perform now. And his future (as well as his health) depend on *that,* not on what he did in the Rose Bowl three years ago.

Similarly, and it may come as a surprise, once you get *your* first job, hardly anyone will ever again care about where you went to high school, attended college, the clubs you were in, the sports you lettered in, even—shock of all shocks—what your grades were. Your day-to-day performance will be the major criteria for keeping your job, getting raises and earning promotions.

Even if we discount the intangible benefits of education— a more complete and fulfilling life, access to more and more interesting people, places and things, etc.—the practical rewards of education can be measured in very real dollars and cents terms. The more you learn, the more you earn.

No Senior Citizen Discounts

A man must always study, but he must not always go to school.

— Montaigne

You will always have to study. Don't believe that when you finally leave school—whether as a dropout or with a PhD— that your days in the classroom and library are over. You will encounter new classrooms throughout your lifetime:

Land any but the most menial job and chances are there will be a training program. The more complicated the job— whether it's primarily manual or professional—the faster and more often you will find yourself back in the classroom. Some training programs at major corporations last for months. Yes, you'll be back in school, whatever your age, and its too late to learn how to study now!

Taking notes? Watch what happens during that first sales meeting when forty new products are flashed on the screen, one right after the other. You'd better be ready to quickly and accurately write down what you need to know to go out and explain them to your prospects. Asking your boss to repeat himself again and again doesn't wash in the real world.

Job promotion? Even if your lack of advanced schooling forced you to start at a clerical or blue collar job, your natural talents might send you up the ladder of success. When that promotion to a white collar job or even a management position does come, you'll be happy to know your company is paying all your expenses for that highly-touted, three-day management training seminar. Yes, it's intense. And yes, you'd better be ready to learn and assimilate the material quickly. And yes, you're back in school again!

The list is endless—birth training sessions, art classes, the entire range of adult education classes, languages, dance, sculpture...whatever interests you, whatever you want or must learn, will require developed study skills. Through all stages of life, opportunities to acquire new knowledge and expand your horizons will constantly present themselves. Will you be ready to take advantage of all those wonderful opportunities?

Master the fundamental study habits, and you'll shout "yes."

How Smart Do *You* Study?

Will this book really help you? Yes, it really will. **How To Study** is the most comprehensive study guide ever written, a fundamental, step-by-step approach that *you* can follow to develop and sharpen your study skills.

If you're struggling through college or graduate school, here's your life raft.

If you're a high school student planning to attend college, hone your study skills *now*.

If you're heading for trade school, planning to dance, write, paint, etc., not considering college, even if you're ready to drop out of high school at the earliest possible instant, you need **How To Study**.

And if you're an adult returning to the classroom after a lengthy absence, there is no substitute for the rules you will learn in this helpful collection of study procedures.

If I Only Had A "C"

What if you're a really poor student?

So what?

How smart you are is not the point. *What counts is how smart you study.*

With the possible exception of those 2% of you who qualify as "gifted," the effective study habits **How To Study** teaches will help students of any age:

If your grades are average to good, you will see a definite difference.

If you are on the borderline of the pass/fail range, you will benefit considerably.

If good study habits are in place but rusty as a result of years away from the classroom, **How To Study** is the perfect refresher for you.

And if you *are* one of those "2% gifted," I *still* think you'll find some helpful techniques in these pages.

Does It Work?

The answer is a resounding yes! One obvious example is the performance of Asian immigrant students in American schools. Hampered by an unfamiliar language, they have nevertheless almost unanimously demonstrated superior academic achievement.

Is it genetic? Something to do with rice? Tropical weather? Monsoons?

No. Studies indicate these students simply excel at incorporating the study ethic—a combination of strong motivation, discipline and a solid adherence to time management—into their everyday lives. And like muscles that are regularly exercised, study skills get stronger and better with practice.

That's what's ahead in **How To Study**. Learning, practicing, honing and strengthening the many skills we'll be discussing in the following pages is no small task. Some will be easier to master than others, yet each plays a definite role in shaping your study habit armament. They are all interrelated, all interdependent, and all must be mastered if the whole is to work effectively. It's a task I'm certain you can accomplish.

Take a day or so off to let the impact of what you can learn—and what it can mean in your life—sink in. Then turn to Chapter 1 and complete your self-evaluation. I think you'll find you already know far more than you think you do!

1

HOW TO

Start
Out
Right

1

> It is not enough to understand what we ought to be, unless we understand what we are; and we do not understand what we are, unless we know what we ought to be.
> — T. S. Eliot

Taking a good, honest look at yourself and rating your own skills is not the easiest thing in the world to do. In the next two chapters, I'm going to help you evaluate the current level of all your study skills—a necessary step to identify the areas in which you need to concentrate your efforts; identify the study environment and learning style that suit you; and categorize all of your school subjects according to how well you like them and how well you do in them.

How To Keep Score

In the next few pages, I'm going to explain the ten primary study skill areas covered in this book: reading, memory development, time management, library skills, textbook note taking, classroom note taking, taking notes in the library, classroom participation, writing papers and test preparation. Then I'm going to ask you to rate yourself on your current level of achievement and understanding of these important skills: "A" for mastery or near mastery of a particular skill; "B" for some mastery; "C" for for little or none. This will enable you to take advantage of your "A" skills, work to improve the "B's," and really concentrate on the "C's."

Remember, there are no right or wrong answers in this assessment—no pass/fail determination. It's only some place to start, a jumping off point from which you can measure your progress and rate those areas in which your skills need improvement.

In order to simplify the process, I've listed the primary study skills on page 23. Take a separate piece of paper and rate yourself on each of the ten skills (from reading to test preparation) *before you read the rest of this chapter.* After you've rated yourself in each area, give yourself two points for every "A," one point for every "B," zero points for every C. If your overall rating is 15 or more, excellent (give yourself an "A"); 10 to 14, good (give yourself a "B"); and if nine or less, fair (give yourself a "C"). Mark this rating under "Initial Study Skills Evaluation."

Now, let's review each of these areas, giving you insight as to what "fair","good" and "excellent" really mean. As you read each section, go ahead and fill in your rating on the chart on page 23...and be honest with yourself. This evaluation will give you a benchmark from which to measure your improvement after you have completed the book. File it away and make the comparison when you've completed reading.

Your Starting Point

Initial Study Skills Evaluation	A ( )	B ( )	C ( )
Reading	A ( )	B ( )	C ( )
Memory Development	A ( )	B ( )	C ( )
Time Management	A ( )	B ( )	C ( )
Textbook Note Taking	A ( )	B ( )	C ( )
Classroom Note Taking	A ( )	B ( )	C ( )
Classroom Participation	A ( )	B ( )	C ( )
Basic Library Skills	A ( )	B ( )	C ( )
Library Note Taking	A ( )	B ( )	C ( )
Writing Papers	A ( )	B ( )	C ( )
Test Preparation	A ( )	B ( )	C ( )
Overall Study Skill Level	A ( )	B ( )	C ( )

Reading

Speed, comprehension and recall are the three important components of reading. Comprehension and recall are especially interrelated—better to sacrifice some speed to increase

23

these two factors. To test your reading and comprehension skills, choose one page from any of your textbooks (not fiction). Read it, close the book and jot down the one, two or more key points made in the selection you read, then review the text and compare your notes with the page. You will get a good idea of how well you understood what you read and just how good your top-of-the-mind recall is.

SCORE: If you can read the material straight through and accurately summarize what you've read, all in less than two minutes, give yourself an "A." If you have some problems reading and understanding the text but are able to complete the assignment in less than five minutes, give yourself a "B." If you are unable to complete the assignment in that time, remember what you read or produce accurate notes at all, give yourself a "C."

Memory Development

Of the basic aptitudes, studies indicate that memory is perhaps the one most susceptible to development. The key, it has been determined, is to repeat the memory sequence of study, then recall. Language students, for example, have been taught to string together sentences in what soon becomes a short story or dialogue. Each day, new words are added and the student is required to remember and "parrot" them back the succeeding day. This add-on process has the effect of both stretching the memory (to make its capacity larger) and exercising it (to make the recall mechanism work more effectively).

Test #1: Look at the number following this paragraph for ten seconds. Then cover the page and write down as much of it as you can remember:

18765433435739586O

24

Test #2: Below are twelve "nonsense" words from a language I just made up and their "definitions." Study the list for 60 seconds in an attempt to remember each word, how it's spelled and its definition:

Cernum	Thigh	**Numnum**	Chew
Erdur	Read	**Daved**	Man
Grendel	Book	**Armer**	Head
Batow	Run	**Hamich**	Elbow
Plitz	Think	**Frecum**	Jacket
Jotto	Kitchen	**Screb**	Twist

Done? Close the book and write down each of the twelve words and its definition. They do not need to be in the order in which they were listed.

SCORE: Test # 1: If you remembered 12 or more digits in the correct order, give yourself an "A," 8 to 12, a "B." 7 or less, give yourself a "C."

Test # 2: If you accurately listed eight or more words and definitions (and that includes spelling my new words correctly), give yourself an "A." If you listed from five to seven words and their definitions or correctly listed and spelled more than eight words but mixed up their definitions, give yourself a "B." If you were unable to remember at least four words and their definitions, give yourself a "C."

Time Management

Your effective use of available study time can be measured by two yardsticks: (1) your ability to break down assignments into component parts (e.g., reading, note taking, outlining, writing) and (2) your ability to complete each task in an efficient manner. The following questions will help you assess how well you are allocating your time, how organized you really are:

A. How many assignments have you failed to complete in the last month because you forgot when they were due, lacked required materials when you needed them or got to the library too late to read the assigned books?

B. Do you have a weekly or monthly calendar?

C. Do you always carry it with you?

D. How much time do you allocate to study each week?

E. How many "all-nighters" (or "near"-all-nighters) did you pull in the last month?

SCORE: A. Give yourself one point for every such assignment; subtract five points if your answer is "none."

B. Add five points for a "no" answer; subtract five points for a "yes."

C. Add two points for a "no;" subtract two for a "yes."

D. Add five points if you don't know; add two points for less than four hours if in high school, less than ten hours if in college; add zero points for less than ten hours in high school, less than twenty hours in college. Subtract one point for scheduled time greater than ten hours in high school, twenty hours in college. Subtract five points if you study that hard but are convinced anyone else would have to study twice as long to accomplish what you do in half the time.

E. Add one point for each all-nighter or near-all-nighter. Subtract one point if "none." Subtract five points if your answer is "none" *and* you're an "A" or ""B" student.

Use the chart on the opposite page to see how you rate and how to grade yourself on this particular skill:

Test Score	Rating	Skill Score
- 22 to - 5	Excellent	A
- 4 to 0	Very good	A
1 - 5	Good	B
6 - 10	Fair	B
11 and up	Poor	C

Library Skills

Using the library is a function of understanding its organization. The more time you spend doing research in a library, the better you will be at it—the easier it will be for you to organize your search and, once you start, to locate the items you need.

Since most libraries are similarly organized, the differences you'll run into between one and another will be primarily due to size. To be considered a "library literate," you should be aware of what kinds of resources are available (books, periodicals, directories, encyclopedias, dictionaries, magazines, newspapers, documents, microfilm files), know how to select and find books (familiarization with the Dewey Decimal System) and be aware of the functions of the library staff.

To better evaluate your library skills, answer the following questions:

A. What collections are restricted in your library?

B. Can you picture in your mind where you would find a biography of Thomas Wolfe in your local library?

C. Where is the reference section in your local library?

D. If you were given the Dewey number for a book, could you find it in less than five minutes?

E. How often have you been to the library in the past six months? The past month?

SCORE: If the answers to these questions are all "obvious" to you, indicating a steady pattern of library use, then you can claim to have the library habit—give yourself an "A." If you can't answer one or more of the above questions or will freely own up to a spotty record of library use, give yourself a "B." If you don't have the faintest clue of where the closest library is, you get a "C."

Note Taking

Three different arenas—at home with your textbooks, in the classroom and at the library—require different methods of note taking.

From Your Textbooks

Working from your books at home, you should highlight or underline key words and phrases or take brief, concise notes in a separate notebook as you read. You should write down questions and answers to ensure your mastery of the material, "starring" those questions to which you *don't* have answers so you can ask them in class.

In Class

Class *preparation* is the key to class *participation*. By reading material to be covered before you come to class, you will be able to concentrate and absorb the teacher's interpretations and points. Using a topical, short sentence approach or your own shorthand or symbolism, copy down only those items which will trigger thematic comprehension of the subject matter. Your notes should be sequential, following the teacher's lecture pattern. When class is completed, review your notes at the first possible opportunity. Fill in the blanks and your own thoughts.

In The Library

What's the difference between taking notes at the library or working at home with library books vs. your own textbooks? Sooner or later you'll have to return library books (if you're allowed to take them out at all), and librarians tend to frown on highlighting them. So you need to have been taught or developed your own system for library note taking. In chapter 7, I'll show you mine.

SCORE: If you feel that your note taking skills are sufficient to summarize necessary data from your textbooks, capture the key points from classroom lectures and discussions and allow you to prepare detailed outlines and write good papers, give yourself an "A". If you feel any one of these three areas is deficient, give yourself a "B." If notes are what you pass to your friends in class, give yourself a "C."

Participating In Class

I don't know too many teachers who don't take each student's class participation into account when assigning grades, no matter how many spot quizzes they pull, how many term papers they assign. And I think you'll find there are teachers out there who will mark down even students who "ace" every paper and quiz if they seem to disappear in the classroom.

SCORE: If you are always prepared for class—which means at the very least reading all assigned material, preparing assigned homework and projects and turning them in when due—actively participate in discussions and ask frequent and pertinent questions as a way of both trumpeting what you already know and filling in the "gaps" in that knowledge, give yourself an "A." If you fail in any of these criteria, give yourself a "B." If you aren't sure where the classroom is, give yourself a "C."

Writing Papers

Writing papers or, for that matter, preparing any sort of report, written or oral, is 90% perspiration (research) and 10% inspiration (writing). In other words, the ability to write a good paper is more dependent on your mastery of the other skills we've already discussed than your mastery of *writing*. If you are an avid reader, familiar with your local library, a good note taker and capable of breaking down the most complex topic into the manageable steps necessary to write a paper, you probably turn in superior papers.

SCORE: If you have given yourself an "A" in Library Skills, Library Note Taking, Time Management and Reading, give yourself an "A." If you feel you turn in relatively good papers but definitely lack in any of these areas, give yourself a "B." If your idea of writing a paper is photocopying the pertinent Cliff Notes and recopying the summary in your own handwriting, give yourself a "C."

Test Preparation

The key to proper test preparation is an accurate assessment of what material will be covered in the examination and what form the test will take. Weekly class quizzes usually cover the most recent material. Midterm and final examinations cover a much broader area—usually all the subject matter to date. Multiple choice tests, essays, lists of math problems, science lab tests all require different preparation and applying

90-0782WAR

different test-taking skills. Knowing the kind of test you're facing will make your preparation much easier.

So will creating your own list of questions you think your teacher will most likely ask. Through periodic review of your text and class notes, the areas in which your teacher is most interested—and on which he or she is most likely to test you—should begin to stand out. As a final "trick," prepare a list of ten or more questions which *you* would ask if the roles were reversed and *you* were the teacher.

SCORE: If you are able to construct tests that are harder than the ones your teacher gives you—and you perform well on those!—give yourself an "A." If you feel you know the material, but somehow don't perform as well as you think you should come test time, give yourself a "B." If you didn't pass your driver's test, let alone algebra, give yourself a "C."

Your Overall Score

Once again, after you've rated yourself in each area, give yourself two points for every "A," one point for every "B," zero points for every C. If your overall rating is 15 or more, excellent (give yourself an "A"); 10 to 14, good (give yourself a "B"); and if nine or less, fair (give yourself a "C"). Put your new score in the section "Overall Study Skills Level" in the chart on page 23.

Now What?

The fact that you have been honest with yourself in evaluating those talents you bring into the study game is a big plus in your favor. Knowing where you are strong and where you need to improve makes everything else a good deal easier. Now, based on your "test" results, why not draw up a list of your assets and liabilities—your areas of strength and weakness? This will focus your attention on those areas which will require the most work to improve. As an example, a typical assessment might look something like this:

STUDY SKILLS BALANCE SHEET

Good	Fair
Time management	Memory development
Library skills	Class participation
Note taking	Reading
Test Preparation	Writing papers

Interpreting Your Results

Assuming for the moment that this is *your* study skills balance sheet, what can we learn from it? Apparently you are relatively organized, familiar with and comfortable using the library, and get a good deal out of classroom lectures, your reading and library research. And you test well...or, at least, prepare well. So some key skills are already in place.

On the other hand, you don't read as much as you should and have trouble comprehending and remembering what you do. Your classroom note taking ability seems to have been developed at the cost of full participation. And your ability to take notes and use the library hasn't yet translated into good papers.

Congratulations! While I would strongly recommend you read the entire book, this simple test has enabled you to identify the chapters you really need to work on—in this case, 3, 5 & 7—and the specific skills that may require work long after you finish reading this book.

Exercise Section

At this stage, you have a pretty good idea of how you rate on the study skills scale. In order to verify your own evaluation, take a few moments to complete the following skills quiz. (Answers on page 183.)

1. Comprehension can be increased through self-testing   T (·) F ( )

2. Recopying notes after class is effective   T (·) F ( )

3. Word association develops memory   T (·) F ( )

4. Comprehension & memory are interrelated   T (·) F ( )

5. Always study in a quiet environment   T (·) F ( )

6. Memory improves with frequent practice   T (·) F ( )

7. Making a list of anticipated test questions is a good idea   T (·) F ( )

8. A detailed outline should be prepared before you begin any library research   T (·) F ( )

9. You should read each assignment twice to understand it better   T (·) F ( )

10. Class notes should be reviewed once a week   T ( ) F (·)

2

HOW TO
Organize Your Studying

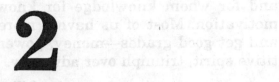

My friend Frank is just entering his junior year of high school. He is bright, though he's never managed better than a "C" average. His school attendance record is spotty, and he'd rather spend "study time" listening to music, cruising with friends or just hanging out. But as he gets closer to senior year and graduation, reality is beginning to snarl in the corner. The tiniest speck of motivation is just beginning to energize his study habits. He has sensed the link between study achievement and jobs and recognizes he will have to earn those things which he wants. The revelation has not transformed him into a scholar. For him studying will always be a means to an end: He doesn't like it, but he recognizes its utility.

Study has become a way to achieve his goals. And that is motivation.

Your pastor or rabbi tells you that "faith can move mountains." Your teachers tell you that wanting to learn, for whatever reason, will almost assure academic success. Few of us are natural-born scholars to whom everything comes easily and for whom knowledge for knowledge's sake is sufficient motivation. Most of us have a more personal reason to study and get good grades—money, power, status, celebrity, competitive spirit, triumph over adversity.

How you view the study skills process—the way in which you understand what you've set out to do—is critical to your success. Approach the process positively—because you have recognized what can be gained from your efforts—and you've already taken that first big step towards achievement. Study skills will be required of you all through your life. Learn them early and well, and they'll serve you well for a long, long time. Remember: A positive attitude and an understanding and belief that good habits can raise your level of performance are your surest guarantee of success.

What Turns *You* On?

Not everybody is highly motivated; many of you may be *barely* motivated. There are two primary factors which act to spur people on—necessity and competition.

The need to provide ourselves with the essentials of life—which does make "necessity the mother of invention"—is what gets most of us out of bed and off to work each morning. If we don't count those cared for by the government and the very rich living on inherited wealth, the rest of us are probably doing something because we *have* to do something.

In our free society, the system is such that anybody can jump into the battle and fight his or her way right to the top. But this very opportunity is what creates competition. And competitors *are* all around us, each seeking to displace us from our rung on the ladder. The point is, however, that it is this freedom to both enter the game and strive for the number one spot—this competitive process—that motivates us. Under this system, each of us *does* have a chance.

Who's Helping Who?

Not everyone gets to use the same starting line in the motivation race. Some of us are luckier than others—we don't have to do it all alone. Three factors that can be essential conditioners of the motivation process are family, school and friends.

Family

A tradition of educational excellence is a key factor in determining which families produce highly motivated students and which add to the truancy rolls. If your father and mother, and their parents before them, have striven, studied, learned and succeeded, they can serve as positive role models for you. In a healthy family situation, it is normal (and expected) for children to outdo their parents. If the family standard is achievement, it's easier to be motivated in that direction.

School

By the time you reach 18, nearly half of your life will have been spent in school. Whether you like it or not. If it were the ideal learning environment, your school would boast teachers who existed solely to impart their knowledge and wisdom, students thirsting to learn and a library spilling over with the books and materials necessary to foster such a process.

If you are lucky enough to find yourself in even a pale imitation of such a school, you will be motivated by both your teachers and peer pressure to achieve: Attend a school with a superior college acceptance rate and aiming for college seems suddenly the logical to do.

On the other hand if you are stuck in a dead-end school, in which crack dealers are more celebrated than scholars, you may well find it hard to convince yourself that a high school education is even worth it. And college isn't even a blip on the horizon.

Friends

The friends we have and the company we keep do much to limit or expand our exposure to learning and culture...and our desire to pursue them.

If you're devoted to "hanging out"—on the athletic field, at rock concerts, on the corner—your chances of visiting a library, museum, art movie or church group diminish accordingly.

Reading is contagious. If you are surrounded by others who read, books will always be your friends. Great works of art are as accessible as the nearest museum. If your friends would tend to suggest a trip to the museum before cruising down Main Street, your cultural palette would quickly become more colorful. You would find you couldn't live without these things in your life, even if you later found yourself surrounded by those who didn't appreciate them as you did.

But as you start out in life, your friends often exert far more influence than your parents or teachers. So even if you are in a great school and come from a highly educated family, the "wrong" crowd can turn your head.

Admittedly, this is a far too brief and simplistic view of the effect these three formative factors have on our lives. But there's an important point to get out of all this: If you have friends, parents and a school all motivating you, be thankful for the "edge" you've been given, for no apparent reason. If you *don't,* it does *not* mean you are a loser or have to accept the cards the Universe seems to have dealt you. You can succeed in spite of your environment—if you want to badly enough. Keep reading. Keep studying. And keep trying.

You will. You can.

You *Can* Get There From Here

Presuming you're ready to motivate yourself—whether or not you have the help of your family, friends or school—just how do you do so? Set your own goals, according to *your* talents and dreams, and reach for the stars!

The development of good study skills is the highway to your goals, whatever they are. And no matter how hard you have to work or how much adversity you have to overcome along the way, the journey will indeed be worth it.

How do you make goal setting a part of your life? Here are some hints I think will help you:

1. *Be realistic.* when you set goals. Don't aim too high or too low and don't be particularly concerned if you wind up having to make adjustments along the way.

2. *Be realistic* about your expectation. An improved understanding of a subject you have little aptitude for is preferable to getting hopelessly bogged down if total mastery of of the subject is just not in the cards.

3. *Beware the Goldilocks Conundrum.* Despite points one and two, you can be *overly* realistic—too ready to sigh and give up just *because* something "isn't in the cards." There's a fine line between aiming too high and feeling miserable when you don't come close, aiming too low and never achieving your potential and finding the path that's right for you.

4. *Concentrate on areas that offer the best chance for improvement.* Unexpected achievement can do wonders for

your confidence and might well make it possible for you to achieve more than you thought in other areas.

5. *Monitor you achievements and keep resetting your goals.* Daily, weekly, monthly, yearly—ask yourself how you've done and where you'd like to go *now.*

Creating *Your* Environment

The time is 8:30 p.m. A U-2 album is on the turntable, and it's cranked up. Your books and notes are strewn across the floor in no particular order. The History test is scheduled for nine the next morning and you haven't looked at the text-book in a week. You've promised your mother you'll take out the garbage and walk the dog. You were up late watching a favorite TV show last night and you're still tired. 8:30 - 10:30 p.m are the hours you've set aside for study.

With all these distractions, the noise level, other commitments and your general fatigue, you're not exactly heading for quality study time. And that's the point: Within such an environment, time spent will most likely be time wasted. How will you concentrate with the loud music? How will you focus on the retention, recognition and recall process when your eyelids are kissing? Will you be called away at a critical moment to walk the dog?

Now imagine the following scenario: You've found a quiet corner at a reading table in your local library. Classes are just over and you review your History notes, still fresh in your mind. You look around you. All heads are down—focusing, concentrating, thinking. This is a *study* environment—you are not separated from the activities of others, but rather a willing participant in a seemingly universal pattern. Now you're ready for *quality* study time. And in half the time you thought it would take, you finish your reading, sift the material, make your notes and head for home.

This comparison of good and bad study environments is so simple as to be self-evident, you'd think. Amazingly, the negative situation portrayed is all too often the case. If it's one *you*'re more familiar with, it's time to make a change. You need the right skills and the right environment if you are to be successful. But the "right" environment for you is probably the "wrong" one for someone else. Do you know where, when and how *you* study best?

In the library? At home? At a friend's?

Before dinner? After dinner?

When's it's quiet? Noisy? With music? In front of the TV?

Easiest assignments first? Hardest first? Reading before writing?

Remember: There are no right or wrong answers. Some of you will require quiet, others music, still others one or the other depending on the subject being studied or the particular task (reading, taking notes, writing a paper, preparing for a test, etc.). What's important is that you find out what works and doesn't work for *you*. You should already have some idea of how, when and where you perform best. If not, take a week and try the whole gamut of times, places and circumstances until you can create your own personal study environment and maximize your effectiveness.

On page 44, I've created a chart on which you can identify the kind of environment in which *you* study best. This includes not just *where* you study—at home, in the library, at a friend's house—but *when* and *how* you study, too. Once you've identified what works for you, avoid those situations in which you now *know* you don't perform best.

My Ideal Study Environment

How I receive information best:

1. ☐ Orally ☑ Visually

In the classroom, I should:

2. ☐ Concentrate on taking notes ☑ Concentrate on listening
3. ☑ Sit in front ☐ Sit in back ☐ Sit near a window or door

Where I study best:

4. ☐ At home ☑ In the library ☐ Somewhere else: _____

When I study best:

5. ☐ Every night; little on weekends ☐ Mainly on weekends ☑ Spread out over seven days
6. ☐ In the morning ☑ In the evening ☐ In the afternoon
7. ☑ Before dinner ☑ After dinner

How I study best:

8. ☑ Alone ☐ With a friend ☐ In a group
9. ☐ Under time pressure ☑ Before I know I have to
10. ☑ With music ☐ In front of TV ☐ In a quiet room
11 ☐ By organizing an entire night's studying before I begin ☑ Tackling and completing one subject at a time

I need to take a break:

12. ☑ Every 30 minutes or so ☑ Every hour ☐ Every 2 hours ☐ Every ____ hours

Many of the items on this chart should be self-explanatory. Why you feel the need for a particular environment isn't really important. Knowing that you *do have a preference* is. Here's what you're trying to assess in each item and how *your* preferences might affect your study regimen:

1. If you prefer "listening" to "seeing," you'll have little problem getting the information you need from class lectures and discussion. In fact, you'll prefer them to studying your textbooks. (You may have to concentrate on your reading skills and spend more time with your textbooks to offset this tendency. Highlighting your texts will help.)

If you're more of a "visual" person, you'll probably find it easier working from your textbook and may have to work on classroom concentration. Taking excellent class notes that you can read later will probably be important for you.

2. This should tie in with your answer to (1). The more "oral" you are, the more you should concentrate on listening. The more "visual," the better your notes should be for later review.

3. This may make a difference for a number of reasons. You may find it difficult to hear or see from the back of the classroom. You may be shy and either want to confront your shyness and sit up front to make yourself participate or sit further back so you can concentrate on the teacher without the anxiety of being too close to call on. You may find sitting near a window makes you feel less claustrophobic; alternatively, you may daydream too much if near a window and should sit as far "in" the classroom as possible!

4. Obvious

5. How to organize your time to most effectively cover the material: This may depend, in part, on the amount of homework you are burdened with and/or the time of year—you may

have one schedule during most of the school year but have to adapt during test time, if papers are due, for special projects, etc.

6. To some of you, such preferences may only be a factor on weekends, because your day hours are set—you're in school. But if you're in college (or in a high school program that mimics college's "choose your own courses and times" scheduling procedures), you would want to use this factor in determining when to schedule your classes. If you study best in the morning, for example, you'd try to schedule as many classes as possible in the afternoons. If you study best in the evening, either schedule classes in the morning and leave afternoons free for other activities, or in the afternoons so you can sleep later (and study later the night before).

7. Some of us get cranky if we try to do anything when we're hungry. If you study poorly when your stomach is growling, eat something!

8. Obvious

9. Just because you perform best under pressure doesn't mean you should always leave projects, papers and studying for tests until the last minute. It just means if you're well organized but an unexpected project gets assigned or a surprise test announced, you won't panic. If you do not study well under pressure, it certainly doesn't mean you occasionally won't be required to. The better organized you are, the easier it will be for you all the time, but especially when the unexpected arises. (Concentrate on time management, chapter 4.)

10. Believe it or not, some of you (like me) will find it difficult to concentrate with*out* music or some sort of noise. Others couldn't sit in front of the TV and do *any*thing but breathe and eat. Many of you will fall in between—you can read and even take notes to music but need absolute quiet to

study for a test or master particularly difficult concepts. If you don't know how you function best, now's the time to find out.

11. Back to organizing. The latter concept—starting and finishing one project before moving on to another—doesn't mean you can't at least sit down and outline an entire night's study plan before tackling each subject, one at a time. Setting up such a study schedule *is* advised. But it may mean you really *can't* move to another project while the one you're now working on is unfinished. Others of you may have no problem working on one project, switching to another when you get stuck or just need a break, then going back to the first.

12. There's nothing particularly wrong with taking a break whenever you feel you need to to keep yourself sharp and maximize your quality study time...as long as the breaks aren't every five minutes and don't last longer than the study periods! In general, though, try to increase your concentration through practice so that you can go at least an hour before getting up, stretching and having a drink or snack. Too many projects will require that long a period to "get into" or organize, and you may find that breaking too frequently will require starting all or nearly over again when you return to your desk.

Da Vincis Are Hard To Find

It is the rare individual who is superior, or even good, in *every* subject. If you are, count your blessings. Most of us are a little better in one subject or another. Some of us simply *like* one subject more than another—and don't think *that* doesn't change your attitude towards it. Others are naturally gifted in one area, average in others.

For example, skill with numbers and spatial relations may come easily to you. but you may have no ear for music or languages. Or you may find learning a language to be easy, but not have the faintest clue why Pythagoras came up with his Theorem...or why you should care. Some students are good with their hands (or, as your career counselor would put it, "exhibit unusual motor skills"). Others (again, like me) may find making the simplest item akin to torture. Well, so I'll never be known as "handy."

The reasons for such unequal distribution of native-born talents lie somewhere in the area between karma and God, depending on your philosophy.

Presuming that most of us are good in one or two subjects, average or poor in others, we can react to this state of affairs in one of two ways: 1) Concentrate on those areas in which we're weakest and work to improve basic skills such as reading, memory and organization so as to minimize our lack of particular talents; or 2) concentrate exclusively on developing the particular skills we feel we like or need without worrying about the others at all.

Most of you would probably lean to the former solution. That's why you're plowing through this book, isn't it? And the skills you will learn, practice and strengthen throughout this book will undoubtedly change your approach to subjects you currently dislike or just aren't good at. It will never enable you to add a string of numbers in your head faster than a calculator or start speaking a language with a near-native accent just by listening to the waiter in the local French restaurant. Unless you are born with those talents. But it may give you the impetus to do better in math or learn French with a little less pain.

On the other hand, each of us has probably met someone who has taken the second course—strengthening his or her native-born talents and ignoring the rest. Such a person— salesman, computer guru, physician, etc.—may have reached an incredible plateau of success in his or her field. While being suitably impressed by their professional accomplishments, we

may be astounded at their demonstrated ignorance of literature, current affairs, art, music or a number of other areas.

Should we criticize this person for concentrating solely
on his or her strengths and doing it so successfully that he or
she becomes a world famous surgeon or the owner of a billion
dollar computer firm? Even if he or she never did do particularly well in English?

It's one way to get where you want to go. And may well
be a path you choose.

A Word Of Caution

Before you agree with the conclusion that only God-given
talents are worthy of development, however, here's some cau-
tionary advice: Pursuit of such a goal can either be a mixed
blessing or a gift in disguise. Logic tells us that things which
come easily, can be easily achieved. Which is not to say that
those areas which require more study cannot be mastered.

My advice is to be thankful for whatever native-born
talents you possess and use their gift as a two edged sword.
Shift some study time from those tasks easily achieved to those
which you find more difficult. The balance you will see in your
development will be well worth the effort.

And if you've never really thought about the subjects you
like and dislike, use the chart on page 50 to identify them.
You'll also be asked to identify those in which you perform well
or poorly. Your report card should confirm your list of those!
Use this list to organize your own schedule to take advantage of
your natural talents and give added time to the subject areas
that need the most work.

Evaluation of Subject Areas

List the subject areas/courses you like most:

engl., writ., art, psych.

List those you like least:

math, sci, hist

List the courses in which you get the best grades:

engl./writing, art

And those in which you get the worst grades:

math, hist., sci.

And If You Have A Choice

All college students—and some high school students—are able to pick and choose courses according to their own schedules, likes, dislikes, goals, etc. The headiness of such freedom should be tempered with the commonsense approach you're trying to develop through reading this book. Here are a few hints to further help you along:

1. Whenever possible, consider each professor's reputation in your ruminations on whether to select a particular course (especially if it is an overview or introductory course that is offered in two or three sessions). Word soon gets around as to which professors' lectures are stimulating and rewarding—an environment in which learning is a joy, even if it isn't a subject you like!.

2. Attempt to select classes so that your schedule is balanced on a weekly and even a daily basis, though this will not always be possible or advisable. (Don't change your major just to fit your schedule!). Try to leave an open hour or half hour between classes—it's ideal for review, post-class note taking, quick trips to the library, etc.

3. Try to alternate challenging classes with those that come more easily to you. Studying is a process of positive reinforcement. You'll need encouragement along the way.

4. Avoid late evening or early morning classes, especially if such scheduling provides you with large gaps of "down time."

5. Set a personal study pace and follow it. Place yourself on a study diet, the key rule of which is: *Don't overeat.* The landscape is littered with the shadows of unsuccessful students who have failed in their pursuits—not because they

lacked the talent or motivation, but because they just over-loaded on information and pressure.

You *can* be successful without killing yourself!

3

HOW TO

Read
And
Remember

3

A review of current testing methods by the two major
players in the college and entrance testing area indi-
cates changes will be coming. The American College
Testing Assessment has concluded that procedures
will be changed to test for more abstract reading skills.
The College Board/SAT will be including new essay
questions, downplaying the current emphasis on multiple choice tests. Most students (about 3 million) aspir-
ing to college entrance will have to take one of these
examinations.

— *New York Times,* Jan. 3, 1989

As an outgrowth of results noted in the National Com-
mission on Excellence In Education study (A Nation At
Risk), the current method of standardized tests (multiple choice) has come under severe criticism. Particular
criticism is aimed at the "fill in the missing letters,
words or sentences" approach we are all familiar with.
The revised testing approach, applicable as early as
grade school, is by learning and reading what children
read and talk about after they have read—in a word,
comprehension.

— *New York Times,* Dec. 7, 1988

Do you get the feeling that all is not what it should be in the world of education? Given the revolutionary shift the above quotes document, it should be easy to see why reading is the very first skill covered in this book: It is, quite simply, *the foundation upon which all of the other skills must build.*

"He is well read." "She's a reader." "It's all in the books." Such oft-quoted references accentuate the value of this amazing process by which we view the written page and sop up knowledge, mood, emotion, facts, story line, etc. Reading transforms and transports us through times past, present and future. Nothing you will do as you pursue your studies will be as valuable as the reading skills you develop, the ultimate long-term learning tool.

How To Read Better

Presuming you agree, what do you do? This chapter will help you learn:

- The "standard" sections of books designed to help you and how to use them
- How to read material the right way (three types of reading)
- How fast (or slow) you should be reading
- How to take better notes in your textbooks and during your reading assignments.
- How to comprehend more of what you read
- How your memory works and what you can do to improve it
- How to build your own library of books and authors

The Shorthand of Reading

There is a group of special sections found in nearly all textbooks and technical materials (in fact, in almost all books except novels) that contain a wealth of information and can help you glean more from your reading. Becoming familiar with this data will enrich your reading experience and often make it far easier. Here's what to look for:

The first page after the title page is usually the *Table of Contents*—a chapter-by-chapter list of the book's contents. Some are surprisingly detailed, listing every major point or topic covered in each chapter.

The first prose section (after the title page, table of contents and, perhaps, acknowledgements page (in which the author thanks other authors and his or her editor, typist, researcher, friends, relatives, teachers, etc., most of which can be ignored by the reader), the *Preface* is usually a description of what information you will find in the book. Authors may also use the preface to point out unique aspects of their book.

The *Introduction* may be in place of or in addition to the preface and may be written by the author or some "name" the author has recruited to lend additional prestige to his or her work. Most introductions are an even more detailed overview of the book—chapter by chapter summaries are often included to give the reader a feel for the material to be covered.

Footnotes may be found throughout the text (a slightly elevated number following a sentence, quote etc. (e.g., "jim dandy"24) and either explained at the bottom of the page on which they appear or in a special section at the back of the text. Footnotes may be used to cite sources of direct quotes or ideas and/or to further explain a point, add information, etc. outside of the text. You may make it a habit to ferret out sources cited in this way for further reading.

If a text tends to use an alarmingly high number of terms with which you may not be familiar, the considerate author will include a *Glossary*—essentially an abridged dictionary that defines, often with examples not used in the text, all such terms.

The *Bibliography*, usually at the end of the book, may include the source material the author used to research the textbook, a list of "recommended reading" or both. It is usually organized alphabetically by subject, making it easy for you to go to your library and find more information on a specific subject.

Appendices containing supplementary data or examples relating to subject matter covered in the text may also appear in the back of the book.

The last thing in a book is usually the *Index*—an alphabetical listing that references, by page number, every mention of a particular name, subject, topic, etc. in the text.

Making it a habit to utilize all of these tools in your text-books can only make your studying easier.

Three Ways To Read

Depending on what you're trying to accomplish in a particular reading assignment and the kind of book involved, there are actually three different ways to read. Knowing when to use each will make any assignment easier:

Quick Reference

This type of reading should be used when seeking specific information or answers to specific questions. It is an attempt to find a road map or set of directions from which clues to solving a problem can be obtained. Subject matter which is heavily structured or formalized will often fall within this category. The following section from <u>Marketing</u> (Prentice-Hall Press, 1977) is a good example of the kind of material which lends itself to quick reference or information gathering. Note the specificity of the data you can derive from it:

"Major hospital needs fall into the following areas:

1. Improved Patient Care: New life-saving products include automatic monitoring devices and warning systems.

2. Saving of Time and Labor: The nurses' non-medical chores can be eased by new equipment. Patients will be able to regulate bed position, heat drapes and television.

3. Speedier Communications and Movement: Products such as two-way radios and conveyor belt systems can improve the functioning of hospitals.

4. The New Hotel Wings: These will be 'self-care centers' for patients. Outside contractors will take charge of meals, laundry and other services".

Study Reading

This second type of reading (often referred to as *critical reading)* is necessary to distinguish thoughts, ideas or concepts—each worthy of, indeed demanding, a critical outlook and analysis—rather than facts. This is the kind of material in which the arguments must add and measure up if the basic principles are to be accepted—you must question it in light of your own experience and knowledge to test its accuracy and pertinence. As an example, review this paragraph from <u>How To Learn</u> (Doubleday. 1961):

"Brawn is growing obsolete. Ever since the end of the eighteenth century, machines have been assuming our physical burdens, freeing us for worthier things. Only recently, it was fashionable to ridicule or, at best, smilingly tolerate the bookworm, the 'egghead', the thinker. No more. We have come to understand the crucial importance of learning. It has become the recognized passport to success in our time, for ours is an age of specialists and experts."

The best way to begin any reading assignment is to skim the pages to get an overall view of what information is included. Then scan and highlight the text and/or take notes in your notebook. See page 64 for further discussion of highlighting.

Newspapers make reading simple—most newspaper articles tend to use the "pyramid" approach. The first paragraph (at the top of the pyramid) makes the major point of the story. Succeeding paragraphs add more and more detail to the story, filling out the pyramid. So gleaning the key news stories from a newspaper is as easy as reading the headlines and the first two or three paragraphs of each.

Your textbooks are not always written to facilitate such an approach, but most of their authors probably make their key point of any paragraph in the first sentence of that paragraph. Succeeding sentences add details. In addition, most of your textbooks include helpful "call outs"—those brief notes or headings in the outside margins of each page that summarize the topic covered in the paragraph or section. Or, like this book, include headings and sub-headings to organize the material.

These standard organizational tools should make your reading job simpler. The next time you have to read a history, geography or similar text, try skimming the assigned pages first. Read the heads, the subheads and the call outs. Read the first sentence of each paragraph. Then go back and start reading the details.

Read one section (chapter, etc.) at a time. And do not go on to the next until you've completed the following exercise:

1. Write definitions of any key terms you feel are essential to understanding the topic being covered.

2. Write questions and answers you feel clarify the topic.

3. Write questions for which you *don't* have answers—then make sure you find them through re-reading, further research or asking another student or your teacher.

4. Even if you still have unanswered questions, move on to the next section and complete numbers 1 - 3 for that section. And so on until your reading assignment is complete.

See if this method doesn't help you get a better handle on any assignment right from the start.

Math and science texts (or any highly technical ones, like economics) require slightly different handling. Steps 1 - 3 should still be followed, though with one addition: Make sure you understand the concepts expressed in the various graphs or charts.

And do *not proceed* to step 4. You must understand one section before moving on to the next, since the next concept is usually based on the previous. If there are sample problems, go and solve those that tie in with the section you have just read to make sure you understand the concepts imparted. If you still fail to grasp a key concept, equation, etc., start again and try again. But *don't* move on—you'll just be wasting your time.

Foreign language texts should be approached the same way, especially basic ones teaching vocabulary. If you haven't mastered the words you're supposed to in the first section, you'll have trouble reading the story at the end of section three, even if you've learned all the words in sections two and three.

So take it one step at a time and make sure you have mastered one concept, vocabulary list, lesson, etc. before jumping ahead.

Aesthetic Reading

> To read a writer is for me not merely to get an idea of what he says, but to go off with him, and travel in his company.
>
> — Andre Gide

This is the fun kind of reading you do for pure enjoyment, for diversion, for the appreciation of a certain literary style or tone. Take the following paragraph from Ann Beattie's popular novel, Falling In Place:

> He was standing with his back to the bed, looking out the window. A week ago, looking out the same window —but early in the morning, not late at night—he had seen a robin teaching her six babies to fly. He had taken one of the shells, an indescribable blue, to New York, to Nina.

There are no "facts" to get from this paragraph. Its tone, though, should move you, for it is the description of a man's love, with all the emotion such a description should include. And that's the "data" you're supposed to get from reading it.

Of course, this is also the kind reading you'll do for any English or Literature course and it requires a different approach than one of your textbooks.

When you're reading any novel, short story, play, etc., approach it first from an aesthetic standpoint: How does it make you feel? What do you think of the characters? Do you like them? Hate them? Relate to them?

Second, make sure you know what's going on—this involves the plot or story line and the development of the characters. On a chapter by chapter basis, you may find it helpful to keep a sheet of paper on which you can jot a sentence or two of the plot development (and, if you wish, characters introduced, etc.). My own note on the first chapter of <u>The Time Machine</u> by H. G Wells might read:

> Time Traveller, Psychologist, the Provincial Mayor, the Medical Man, a Very Young Man and Filby are in the Time Traveller's house. It is a winter evening (fire is going). They talk about the geometry of Four Dimensions—4th dimension is time. TT declares he has discovered way to move about in Time and shows them experimental verification—small model for Time Machine (took two years to make) that disappears when activated. Claims it is travelling in time. Announces that big machine is nearly ready and that, when finished, he will use it for a journey in Time. Shows them machine.

I have written these notes out, but obviously you would not need to do so. Simply listing the points in outline fashion or noting key words would be sufficient for many of you.

Does this adequately summarize the first chapter so you wouldn't have to read it? Not really. Yes, it tells you the characters introduced and, in bare bones fashion, what happened. But it leaves out all of the details of the philosophical debate that begins the book and, most importantly, cannot possibly capture the mystery, foreboding and thrill of entering an adventure that Wells manages to convey in this single chapter. And it leaves out important information like the themes carried out in the book, use of literary devices, etc. To truly summarize this chapter, you might label the above paragraph "Plot" and then include separate notes under the headings "Themes" and "Literary." This would certainly help you both understand what you've read and simplify your review task come test time.

Take Out The Crayolas

If you have a desk drawer full of magic markers *(aka highlighters)*, you're probably already familiar with the process of underlining text. It's a useful method for zeroing in on what's important, both during the classroom preparation stage (reading) and when you're compiling your notes. Here's what you should know about the process.

1. Underlining or highlighting your texts are efficient ways to emphasize areas you don't feel comfortable with.

2. Underlining should identify words or sentences that capsulize a section's major ideas or themes.

3. Underlining should indicate the relative importance of things, allowing you to concentrate your review time on key words, facts and concepts (underlined) and skip the digressions, examples and extraneous explanations (not underlined).

4. Underlining classroom notes is an excellent way to suggest that like material should be re-read in the text.

To sharpen your underlining skills, read though the next three paragraphs from another of my books, Internships, Volume I, and indicate with your highlighter which sentences you would color:

For the most part, young people entering the field do not understand just what public relations involves or how to employ public relations techniques to address a communications issue. Some think it involves just dealing with the press. Others think it is mostly writing. Still others are sure that what*ever* it is, it's involved somehow with impacting public opinion, but then confuse it with advertising.

In fact, public relations might be defined in many ways. *Webster's New World Dictionary* defines it as "those functions of a corporation concerned with informing the public of its activities, policies, etc., and attempting to create favorable public opinion." Other texts have used slightly different definitions.

We tell anyone interested in public relations that the best way to understand the field...is to intern in either a public relations firm or a corporate communications department of a major company. This will give you firsthand experience and exposure to the many varied facets of public relations *before* you have to commit yourself to the field."

It should be obvious that the definition of public relations is the essence of the first two paragraphs. You'll want to remember "those functions of a corporation ... favorable public opinion." Highlight that entire definition. (If this were in one of your textbooks, you may want to write in the margin "PR: def" (inition) as a way of catching your attention and moving your eye to this important information.

Secondly, you may highlight the word "intern" or even the whole phrase "best way to understand the field is to intern," the key point in the third paragraph.

Now if you had to review that book for a test, you would glance at two sentences—the two you highlighted—to get the gist of three paragraphs. It will save you tremendous time.

How Fast Can You Understand?

Are you worried that you read too slowly? You probably shouldn't be—less-rapid readers are not necessarily less able. What's counts is what you comprehend and remember. And like anything else, practice will probably increase your speed levels. If you must have a ranking, take any randomly selected text of 200 words and read it from start to finish, noting the elapsed time on your watch. Then score yourself as follows:

Under 25 seconds	Very Fast
26-40 secs.	Fast
41-55 secs	Average
56-70 secs.	Slow
71+ secs.	Very Slow

You should only worry—and plan to do something about it—if you fall in the slow or very slow range. Unless you do, you are probably reading as fast as you need to. Again, the relationship between your reading speed and your comprehension is paramount: Read too fast and you may comprehend less; reading slowly does not necessarily mean you're not grasping the material. There are several things you can do to improve these reading mechanics:

To Increase Your Reading Speed

1. Focus your attention and concentration.

2. Eliminate outside distractions

3. Provide for an uncluttered, comfortable environment.

4. Don't get hung up on single words or sentences, but *do* look up (in the dictionary) key words that must be understood to grasp an entire concept.

5. Try to grasp overall concepts rather than attempt to understand every detail.

To Increase Comprehension:

1. Try to make the act of learning sequential—comprehension is built by adding new knowledge to existing knowledge.

2. Review and re-think at designated points in your reading. Test yourself to determine if the import of the material is getting through to you.

3. If things don't add up, discard your conclusions. Go back, reread and try to find an alternate conclusion.

When we read too fast or too slowly, we understand nothing.
— Pascal

Most importantly, read at the speed that's comfortable for you. Though I *can* read extremely fast, I *choose* to read novels much more slowly so I can appreciate the author's word play. Likewise, any material that I find particularly difficult to grasp slows me right down. On the other hand, I read newspapers, popular magazines and the like very fast, seeking to grasp the information but not worrying about their "literary aspects" or remembering every detail.

Should you take some sort of "speed reading" course, especially if your current speed level is slow? The slower you read, the *less* I recommend such a course. Better to take a course and learn how to read faster while mastering the basics of good reading habits. After (or if you've already) achieved a reasonable level of speed, I see nothing wrong with taking any such course. I can't see that it can particularly hurt you in any way. I can also, however, recommend that you simply keep practicing reading, which will increase your speed naturally.

Remembering What You Read

In a world where the ability to master and remember a growing explosion of data is critical for individual success, too little attention is paid to the dynamics of memory and systems for improving it. Developing your memory is probably the most effective way to increase your efficiency, in reading and virtually everything else. So a brief overview of the memory function —especially its three key aspects—is important.

Retention

Retention is the process by which we keep imprints of past experiences in our minds, the "storage depot." Subject to other actions of the mind, what is retained can be recalled when needed.

Things are retained in the same order in which they are learned. So your studying should build one fact , one idea, one concept upon another.

Broad concepts can be retained much more easily than details. Master the generalities and the details will fall into place.

If you think something is important, you will retain it more easily. An attitude which says, "I *will* retain this," *will* help you remember. So convincing yourself that what you are studying is something you must retain (and recall) increases your chances of adding it to your storehouse.

Recall

This is the process by which we are able to bring forth those things which we have retained. Recall is subject to strengthening through the process of repetition. ***Recall is least*** *effective immediately after a first reading,* emphasizing the importance of review. The dynamics of our ability to recall are affected by several factors.

We most easily recall those things which are of interest to us.

Be selective in determining how much you need to recall. All things are not of equal importance—focus your attention on being able to recall the most *important* pieces of information.

Allow yourself to react to the data you are studying. Being able to associate new information with what you already know will make it easier to recall.

Repeat, out loud or just in your mind, what you want to remember. Find new ways of saying those things that you want to recall.

Try to recall broad concepts rather than isolated facts.

Use the new data you have managed to recall in a meaningful way, which will help you recall it the next time.

Recognition

This is the ability to see new material and recognize it for what it is and what it means. Familiarity is the key aspect of recognition—you will feel that you have "met up" with this information before, associate it with other circumstances and then recall the framework in which it logically fits.

If you've ever envied a friend's seemingly wondrous ability to recall facts, dates, telephone numbers, etc. virtually at will, take solace that, in most cases, *this skill is a result of study and practice,* not something anyone is born with.

There are certain fundamental memory systems that, when mastered, can significantly expand your capability. It is beyond the scope of this book to teach you some or all of these detailed techniques, but if you feel you need help, why not consult your local library? I personally recommend a best seller from a few years ago called <u>The Memory Book</u> by Harry Lorayne and Jerry Lucas, but I'm sure you'll find a number of helpful titles at your library.

Test Your Reading Comprehension

Remember: Comprehending what you read is, to a great extent, more important than how fast you read it. The following section will test your reading comprehension. The first selection is the easiest, the other two are progressively more difficult. Read each selection carefully, then answer the questions. And note that there is not necessarily a single right answer for each question, only one closest to the truth.

Fiction (Least Difficult)

David approached the house slowly. An attitude of caution overcame him as without prior knowledge, just what he could expect to find was problematic. Communications with the old man and woman had been sparse and in recent years very few words of their welfare had come to the family.

Economic conditions in that part of the world were just beginning to stabilize. The first Great War and now this revolution cast a doubt on one's ability to eke out even the most meager of existences. He had come prepared with a gift of dollars which he knew would help to guarantee their welfare.

Finally he arrived at the door and in a moment the three of them embraced. Strange, he thought, how the bonds of family could bridge oceans. Immediately he realized he belonged and that his long journey had indeed been the right thing to do."

Questions (choose only one answer)

1. In this fictional account, the writer's primary purpose is to:

    A. Give the reader a view of economic conditions
    B. Describe the difficulties of meeting long-lost relatives
    C. Emphasize the bonds of family that remain regardless of circumstance
    D. Pad the book by another page
    E. Demonstrate that virtue is its own reward

2. Where is the book set?

    A. Asia
    B. The United States
    C. Unknown
    D. Not the United States
    E. Heaven

3. What relation is David to the people he is visiting?

    A. They are his parents
    B. They are his grandparents
    C. They are family friends
    D. They are relatives
    E. They are people he met on the Road to Morocco

History (More Difficult)

Franklin Delano Roosevelt's chief accomplishments encompass both domestic and international activities.

First elected when the country suffered a severe economic collapse, he was instrumental in mobilizing the nation's people and resources to spearhead a recovery. In present-day economic terms, he presided over the greatest turnaround in the nations' history.

Applying the full weight of central government, he established the principle of government as the court of last resort. Specifically this welfare approach included: the establishment of Social Security; a variety of "make-work" projects that created millions of jobs; federally guaranteed insurance on depositors' bank accounts; stock market regulation; rural power and electrification; the establishment of minimum wage and working conditions standards; and unemployment insurance.

During World War II, FDR presided over the largest military buildup and subsequent engagement ever faced by the nation. He was the successful Commander-In-Chief directing the military forces of the nation in a global encounter with the forces of Fascism and Expansionism.

Roosevelt early on recognized the threat which the Axis powers presented and mobilized the country— primarily by helping to arm England via the mechanism of Lend-Lease—against them. There were those, and many in high places, who sought to minimize the American role in the impending war. Roosevelt, however, was accurate in his belief in the inevitability of U.S. involvement. He recognized the ultimate threat to American freedom which Fascism represented. When the Japanese attack on Peal Harbor made war a *fait accompli*, Roosevelt was ready.

Roosevelt's wartime stewardship demonstrated, as it had during the Depression, his genius for leadership. His words mobilized the nation. His efforts, together with those of Churchill and Stalin, led the Free World to victory.

Some revisionist historians would argue that postwar activities (started at the Yalta Conference) jeopardized America's postwar influence, particularly in Eastern Europe. It seems more logical to assume the Cold War rivalry which exists to this day was a natural outgrowth of two antithetical systems, each feeling heady with victory, each determined to make their manner of governing the law of the land.

Roosevelt's place in history is assured. Though himself privileged by birth, he displayed an unusual compassion for the average man. A non-combatant because of his illness, he demonstrated a courage and leadership which stood as a fine example for battlefield troops.

Questions

1. The writer's main purpose in this selection is to:

   A. Describe world conditions during FDR's presidency.
   B. Demonstrate Roosevelt's grasp of both domestic and international problems.
   C. Indicate that leadership is essential for an effective presidency.
   D. Indicate the broad scope of programs developed to reinvigorate a depressed economy.
   E. Emphasize the inevitability of confrontation between countries with different forms of government.

2. The author asserts that Roosevelt:

   A. Provided necessary leadership in turning the economy around.
   B. Did not hesitate to involve government.
   C. Was the grandfather of the welfare state.
   D. Pioneered many social reforms and make-work programs.

3. One can conclude that Roosevelt:

   A. Understood the real threat posed by Fascism.
   B. Was able to marshal the necessary cooperation among allies for the conduct of a successful global war effort.

C. Understood the necessity to arm England.

D. Was not anxious for war but realistic about its possibility.

4. The phrase "postwar influence" refers directly to:

A. Agreement on spheres of power determined at Yalta.

B. An acknowledgement of the military realities when hostilities ceased.

C. The recognition of the competing natures of Democracy and Communism.

D. A permanent division of the world along superpower lines.

Current Events (Most Difficult)

The problem of the budget deficit will probably be one of the most difficult (and politically thorny) which the new Bush Administration will have to face.

Deficits in Federal budgets arise when expenditures exceed revenue receipts. The difference is considered the deficit.

Deficits cause problems because the dollars required to cover such budgetary shortfalls have to be borrowed. As on any loan, interest payments on the amount borrowed must also be made (debt service). With an annual deficit in the $100-200 billion range, it's easy to see how costly and non-productive such debt service payments can become.

Budget deficits are not a new problem and, some say, not even an important one. These latter optimists argue that the U. S. budget deficit is not the highest of all nations in the West, and, with everything being relative, it is not, therefore, a vital threat. Whether or not you agree with this rosy scenario, the political impetus to reduce the deficit and ultimately live within our means is underway. Congress has crystalized this process by passing the Gramm-Rudman Act, a bill which mandates across-the- board budget cuts to meet certain deficit reduction targets. This is the law of the land, and it will be automatically exercised unless minimum reductions are effected voluntarily.

There are two favorite approaches now in play with respect to this balancing act:

1. <u>Growth:</u> This theory posits that the economy will grow with sufficient vigor to bring in sufficient increases in tax revenues to cover the shortfall.

2. <u>Spending</u> <u>Cuts:</u> Extensive cuts in social and military budgets, coupled with greater income tax revenues, will be required to cover the deficit.

The Administration has complicated the negotiating process between Congress and the Executive Branch with its campaign pledge to refrain from any new taxes. Read his lips.

The outlook is for a lengthy debate and, hopefully, some compromise agreement between the protagonists. Most political experts expect the process to go down to the wire, just shy of the Gramm-Rudman deadline.

Public opinion soundings indicate that, given a compelling case for the imposition of new taxes, the public is more willing to pay additional taxes than Congress is to push them.

Questions

The author characterizes budget deficits as:

A. An unambiguous danger to the economy
B. A subject of controversy and divided opinion
C. The target of political jockeying
D. Subject to adjustment

2. It is obvious from this reading that:

    A. Negotiating in good faith will be important
    B. Graham-Rudman is a popular option
    C. Military cutbacks are on the table
    D. Bush's "no new taxes" pledge may backfire

3. Growing out of a deficit position:

    A. Is an optimist's point of view
    B. Threatens inflation
    C. Can be part of the solution
    D. Depends on realistic forecasting

4. People are willing to pay increased taxes:

    A. Reluctantly
    B. If a legitimate case can be made for them
    C. If they are progressive
    D. If they think they will get something in return

5. Budget deficits are:

    A. Like paying off a loan
    B. Non-productive *vis a vis* the interest paid on them
    C. An operating fact of life for most nations
    D. Possibly not be a bad thing at all

Now check your answers on page 183. This is the kind of testing material you'll come upon again and again, and practice does make perfect. If you didn't get at least nine of these dozen questions right, work on your memory skills and start highlighting text as you read to make comprehension of the main points easier.

As nice as getting the right answers is, it's also important that you are reading and comprehending the material efficiently. Did you have to read the entire text of each selection more than once in order to get the meaning? Did you find yourself reading more slowly than usual in order to comprehend the complexities of the material? Did it take you more than three minutes to read any of the texts?

If you answered "yes" to *any* of these questions, stop patting yourself on the back and start working on the area you obviously still need to improve—comprehension *with* speed.

Read On

In so far as one can in a single chapter, I've tried to sum up the essentials of reading. It is not a finite science but rather a skill and appreciation that one can develop over time. Early good grade school training is essential. And for those of you who have been able to identify problem areas, there are always remedial classes.

Having a "love affair" with books is the best boost you can give yourself. Reading is active, not passive. To paraphrase a guru of my generation: Turn on, tune in, read a book.

Build A Library

The reading of all good books is like conversation with the finest men of past centuries.
— Descartes

If you are ever to become an active, avid reader, access to books will do much to cultivate the habit. We suggest you build your own library. Your selections can and should reflect your own tastes and interests, but try to make your selections wide and varied. Include some of the classics, contemporary fiction, poetry and biography. And save your high school and college texts. You'll be amazed at how some of the material retains its relevance. And try to read a good newspaper every day so as to keep current and informed.

Your local librarian can refer you to any number of lists of the "Great Books," most of which are available in inexpensive paperback editions. Here are three more lists—my own—of: 1) the "great" classical authors; 2) the "great" not-so-classical (i.e., mainly 19th & 20th century) authors, poets and playwrights; and 3) a selection of my own "great books" (generally contemporary, not classics like Virgil's *Aeneid* or Homer's *Odyssey)*. You may want to incorporate these on your buy list, especially if you're planning a summer reading program.

(Note: Most people will not take great issue with the classical authors—they're relatively standard. I have undoubtedly, however, left off someone's favorite author and/or "important" title. So be it. The lists are not meant to be comprehensive, just relatively representative. And I doubt that anyone would disagree that someone familiar with the majority of authors and works listed would be considered well-read!)

Some "Great" Classical Authors

Boccaccio	Confucius	S. Johnson	Flaubert
Burke	Emerson	Kant	Spinoza
Aesop	Dante	Homer	Rousseau
Aquinas	Descartes	Horace	Shakespeare
Cervantes	Machiavelli	Nietzsche	Aristophanes
Chaucer	Goethe	Plato	Vergil
Aristotle	Dewey	Aeschylus	Santayana
J. Caesar	Erasmus	Milton	Swift
Balzac	Hegel	Montaigne	Pindar
Cicero	Ovid	Plutarch	Voltaire

Some Other "Great" Authors

Albert Camus
Aldous Huxley
Alexandr I. Solzhenitsyn
Alexandre Dumas
Anthony Burgess
Arthur Conan Doyle
Bertolt Brecht
Bertrand Russell
Brendan Behan
Carl Sandburg
Charles Dickens
Charles Lamb
Charlotte Bronte
Daniel Defoe
D. H. Lawrence
Dylan Thomas
e e cummings
Edgar Allan Poe
Edward Albee
Ellery Queen
E. M. Forster
Emile Zola
Emily Bronte
Emily Dickinson
Erich Maria Remarque
Ernest Hemingway
Eugene O'Neill
Ezra Pound
F. Scott Fitzgerald
Fyodor Dostoevsky
George Bernard Shaw
George Eliot
George Orwell

George Sand
Gertrude Stein
Henry Miller
Henry Wadsworth Longfellow
Hermann Hesse
Herman Melville
H. G. Wells
H. H. Munro (Saki)
H. L. Mencken
Isaac Asimov
James Baldwin
James Jones
James Joyce
James Russell Lowell
James Thurber
J. D. Salinger
Jean Paul Sartre
John Galsworthy
John Hersey
John Keats
John Updike
Jose Ortega y Gasset
Joseph Conrad
Joseph Heller
J. R. R. Tolkien
Kahlil Gibran
Leo Tolstoy
Lewis Carroll
Lord Byron
Marcel Proust
Mark Twain
Maxim Gorky
Nathaniel Hawthorne

O. Henry
Oscar Wilde
Pearl Buck
Percy Bysshe Shelley
P. G. Wodehouse
Robert Frost
Robert Heinlein
Robert Louis Stevenson
Robert Penn Warren
Rudyard Kipling
Samuel Beckett
Saul Bellow
Sinclair Lewis
Tennessee Williams
Theodore Dreiser
Thomas Hardy
Thomas Mann
Thomas Wolfe

Thornton Wilder
Truman Capote
T. S. Eliot
Upton Sinclair
Victor Hugo
Vladimir Nabokov
Walt Whitman
Washington Irving
W. H. Auden
William Blake
William Butler Yeats
William Faulkner
William James
William Styron
William Wordsworth
W. Somerset Maugham

Some "Great" Works

1) A Long Day's Journey Into Night
3) A Portrait of the Artist as a Young Man
5) A Streetcar Named Desire
7) Aesop's Fables
9) All Quiet On The Western Front
11) Arrowsmith
13) Babbitt
15) Brave New World
17) Catch-22
19) Grapes of Wrath
21) Death of a Salesman
23) The Great Gatsby
25) Don Quixote
27) Wuthering Heights

2) Animal Farm
4) Tom Jones
6) Look Homeward, Angel
8) Alice In Wonderland
10) An American Tragedy
12) Canterbury Tales
14) The Bell Jar
16) The Brothers Karamazov
18) Remembrance of Things Past
20) Don Juan
22) The Deerslayer
24) Lord Jim
26) The Legend of Sleepy Hollow
28) Ethan Fromme

29) Far From the Madding Crowd

30) A Farewell to Arms

31) Gulliver's Travels

32) Hamlet

33) Huckelberry Finn

34) The Iliad

35) Kim

36) The Old Man and the Sea

37) Leaves of Grass

38) Les Miserables

39) MacBeth

40) Main Street

41) The Merchant of Venice

42) Moby Dick

43) Native Son

44) 1984

45) Of Human Bondage

46) Of Mice and Men

47) Oliver Twist

48) The Pickwick Papers

49) One Flew Over the Cuckoo's Nest

50) Othello

51) Our Town

52) War and Peace

53) Paradise Lost

54) Anna Karenina

55) Robinson Crusoe

56) Scarlet Letter

57) Siddhartha

58) The Magic Mountain

59) Silas Marner

60) Lady Chatterly's Lover

61) Steppenwolf

62) Demian

63) Tender Is the Night

64) Pride and Prejudice

65) The Catcher in the Rye

66) Bonfire of the Vanities

67) The Count of Monte Cristo

68) Crime and Punishment

69) The Federalist

70) For Whom the Bell Tolls

71) The Foundation

72) The Thin Red Line

73) The Good Earth

74) "The Road Less Travelled"

75) The Hound of the Baskervilles

76) David Copperfield

77) The Idiot

78) King Lear

79) The Invisible Man

80) Jane Eyre

81) The Lord of the Rings

82) The Prophet

83) The Raven

84) Mother Courage

85) The Red Badge of Courage

86) Return of the Native

87) The Sun Also Rises

88) Tale of Two Cities

89) The Time Machine

90) The Aeneid

91) "The Wasteland"

92) The Trial

93) Tom Sawyer

94) Romeo and Juliet

95) Ulysses

96) Man and Superman

97) Vanity Fair

98) Walden

99) Heart of Darkness

100) Julius Caesar

Reading every one of these books will probably make you a better reader; it will certainly make you more well-read. And that is the extra added bonus to establishing such a reading program—an appreciation of certain authors, certain books, certain cultural events and the like is what separates the cultured from the merely educated and the undereducated.

Exercises

1. How many of the 40 "classical" authors listed on page 78 are you familiar with (i.e., their names "ring a bell")?

2. How many of these classical authors have you actually read?

3. How many of the 100 authors listed on pages 79 & 80 have you read?

4. How many of the books listed on pages 80 & 81 have you read?

5. Can you list the author of each of the books listed on pages 80 & 81?

(See pages 183 - 185 for answers and ratings.)

4

HOW TO

Organize Your Time

4

Tempus fugit

Translation: Time Flies (or, at the very least, drives a fast car)

In the many books and articles devoted to "efficiency," the most-overused, misunderstood and probably overblown word is "management." This latest buzzword (yes, there is "time management") has assumed a life of its own. It's even taken on, especially for the many gurus that seem to exist only on late-night cable TV, the aura of some magical elixir: Just wave a wand, invoke your "management skills" and all tasks will miraculously fall in place. Nothing could or should be further from the truth, which is far simpler.

Most so-called time management systems tend to be so complex that their mastery and execution often dwarf the material to be mastered. This chapter does not propose yet another system. Instead, I've offered just two very basic tools you will find immensely helpful and details on the various organizational habits, tricks and techniques I've learned and applied over the years.

Goal setting is a key step in the effective use of time: The more you want to accomplish a task and the more intent you are on reaching your objective, the easier it is to do so. All of the techniques of time organization are simply tools to help you reach your destination with minimum effort, maximum efficiency and the fewest wrong turns.

Simple common sense is your best ally when you need to achieve certain tasks within a pre-determined period of time. Trial and error will help you to adapt the tools I'm going to give you in this chapter into your own personal organizational system, one that will not overpower the tasks you're trying to accomplish or take you until graduation to master.

The Time Has Come Today

Like virtually all of the skills discussed in this book, learning how to become more efficient—how to accomplish more tasks in less time—is a habit that will benefit you throughout your lifetime, not just while you're trying to make it through English 4 or Chem 203.

Why? Well, the more efficiently you accomplish things you aren't particularly fond of, the more time you will have to do the things you really enjoy. For example, I am not particularly fond of shopping. So when I have to do it, I make a point of organizing my trip—five minutes spent making a list of what I have to buy and an efficient route to the stores. The result? I probably spend half the time shopping than I would if I just jumped in the car with no plan in mind. And when I'm done shopping, I have extra time to devote to my hobbies.

Remember what I've stressed throughout this book: The object is not for you to devote *more* time to studying (unless, of course, you're only visiting your books once a month or so); it's to devote the same or even *less* time to studying but accomplish *more*. Wouldn't you rather be out on a date than cramming for a test?

Asking The Right Question

The *wrong* questions: How organized (or disorganized) are you now? How organized do you *want* to be? How organized *should* you be?

The *right* question: How organized do you *need* to be.

If you're already well-organized—if you greet each of the ideas, hints and tools in this chapter as old friends—fine, pick up what you can use and move on.

Now for the rest (most) of you. If you're chronically disorganized, never have the right books with you, always have to cram for major tests hours before they're given, always get to the library too late to check out the book you need (that night, of course) or have a killer class load and/or a heavy work or activity schedule—*you don't really have much a choice, do you?* You can continue to miss assignments, get poor grades and be late to and for everything, or you can say enough is enough, use the simple tools in this chapter and change your life.

What's It All About?

There's a simple *what, how* and *why* cycle to which most time management systems can be reduced:

1. Determine *what* you want to achieve and how much time is available to do it.

2. Determine *how* you expect to achieve your goals given the realities of time wasting which we all fall prey to.

3. Determine *why* you are doing certain things (and not others) and see if your activities are in sync with your overall plans.

Now that you know what we're trying to accomplish together, here are are two basic tools which will change your habits forever.

The Project Board

Your day-to-day activities—classes, appointments, regular daily homework assignments, daily or weekly quizzes, etc. —will be dealt with in the next section. In this section, I want to talk about those projects (including studying for mid-term and final exams) that require completion over a long period of time. Weeks. Maybe months.

For such long-term tasks—term papers, studying for major exams, etc.—it's imperative to create a chart that you can keep on your wall at home to keep track of the various steps involved.

I have termed such a chart "The Project Board" and reproduced a sample of one—containing details on two projects and exams for four classes—on pages 90 & 91. (It is not necessary for you to construct your own Project Board, though it is certainly the least expensive alternative. There are ready-made charts for professionals [yes, you're learning something that you can use throughout your life—professionals call it a flow chart] available in a variety of formats—magnetic, erasable, utilizing note cards. Your local art supply, stationery or book store may have a selection of such items for purchase.)

How does it work? As you can see, it is really nothing but a calendar, albeit a "looser" one than you'll be constructing in the next section. I have set it up vertically—that is, the months running down the left-hand side, the projects across the top. It is certainly no problem to switch and have the dates across the top and the projects running vertically. It all depends on what space you have on your wall.

In the case of each project, there is a key preparatory step before you can use the chart—you have to break down each general assignment into its component parts, the specific tasks involved in any large project. So, for example, in the case of the English report on Dante, we have identified the steps as: 1) Finalize topic; 2) Initiate library research; 3) Prepare general outline; 4) Do detailed library research; 5) Prepare detailed outline (from note cards); 6) Write first draft; 7) Do additional research (if necessary); 8) Write second draft; 9) Spell check and proofread 10) Get someone else to proofread 11) Type final draft. 12) Proofread again. (These steps, with some minor variations along the way, are common to virtually any written or oral report or paper. For further discussion of them, see chapter 7) Next to each specific task, we have estimated the time we would expect to spend on it.

The second project involves working on a team with other students from your entrepreneurship class on creating a hypothetical student business. While the steps are different, you'll notice that the concept of breaking the project down into separate and manageable steps and allocating time for each doesn't change. However, since time allocation in later steps depends on exactly what assignments you're given by the group, we have had to temporarily place question marks (?) next to some steps. As the details of this project become clearer and specific assignments are made, your Project Board should be changed to reflect both more details and the specific time required for each step.

Sample Projects Board

MONTH/WEEK		PROJECT: STUDENT CORPORATION
1st MONTH	Week 1	Initial group meeting: Discuss overall assignment and possible products or services—bring list of three each to meeting (1 hour)
	Week 2	Finalize product or service; finalize organization of group and longterm responsibilities of each subgroup. (3)
	Week 3	Subgroup planning and short-term assignments (2)
	Week 4	Work on individual assignment from subgroup (?)
2nd MONTH	Week 1	Work on individual assignment from subgroup (?)
	Week 2	Work on individual assignment from subgroup (?)
	Week 3	Integrate individual assignment with rest of subgroup (?)
	Week 4	Meet with entire group to integrate plans (?)
3rd MONTH	Week 1	Finalize all-group plan; draft initial report (?)
	Week 2	Type and proof final report (?)
	Week 3	
	Week 4	
	DUE DATE	3RD MONTH/end of Week 2

PROJECT: DANTE TERM PAPER	REVIEW/EXAM SCHEDULE
Finalize topic (1 hour)	Review prior month's History notes (3)
Initial library research (2) General outline (1)	Review prior month's English notes (2)
Detailed library research (3)	Review prior month's Science notes (4)
Detailed library research (3)	Review prior month's Math notes (4)
Detailed library research (3)	Review 1st MONTH History notes (3)
Detailed outline (1)	Review 1st MONTH English notes (2)
First draft (4), Additional research (2)	Review 1st MONTH Science notes (4)
	Review 1st MONTH Math notes (4)
Second draft, spellcheck, proof (10)	2nd MONTH History notes (3)
Independent proof (1)	2nd MONTH English notes (2)
	2nd MONTH Science notes (4)
Type final draft and proof (4)	2nd MONTH Math notes (4)
end of 3RD MONTH	end of 3RD MONTH

The last item on your new Project Board is studying for *all* your final exams—in History, English, Math and Science. If you have skipped ahead and read chapter 8, you know that cramming for tests doesn't work very well in the short term and doesn't work at *all* over the long term. So you have taken my advice in that chapter and made it a habit to review your class notes on each subject on a monthly basis. (I've slightly altered reality to make it convenient to allocate such time— four subjects, four weeks per month.) You've simply decided that every Sunday morning is "review time" and allocated one Sunday a month to review the previous month's work in each subject.

As a result of this plan, you'll notice there is little time allocated to "last minute" cramming or even studying for a specific final the week before it is given—just a couple of hours to go over any details you're still a little unsure of or to spend on areas you think will be on the test. While others are burning the midnight oil in the library the night before each exam, you're getting a good night's sleep and will enter the tests refreshed, relaxed and confident. Seems like a better plan to me.

As a by-product of this study schedule, by the way, you will find that salient facts and ideas will remain with you long after anybody is testing you on them.

Now that you have your Project Board, what do you do with it?

Continue to revise it according to actual time spent as opposed to time allocated. Getting into this habit will make you more aware of what time to allocate to future projects and make sure that the more you do so, the more accurate your estimates will be.

Incorporate all of these projects and the necessary time into your weekly calendar.

Your Weekly Calendar

This is your major organizational tool—a weekly calendar, preferably one that is always with you, on which you faithfully enter:

1) The time, location and materials needed for every class and every appointment (social or otherwise).

2) All extracurricular activities—sports, clubs, etc.— both times and locations for meetings and projects/ assignments to accomplish.

3) Time allocated for study each day

4) Daily/weekly assignments to be completed during each day's study time

5) Materials (stationery, books, notes, etc.) needed for each day's assignments

6) Additional tasks from your Projects Board to be completed during that day's study time

7) Break times

8) Any non-study chores that must be completed

9) Anything else you want to write down if doing so will make you be or even just feel more organized, less harried, more efficient.

On pages 94 & 95, I've reproduced just three days from what I think your weekly calendar would look like if you're a reasonably active college student. You'll notice it is relatively full. But it is also difficult for a student with this calendar to miss a class or assignment, forget an appointment or not buy a present for Aunt Clara's birthday. And that is the idea of the calendar—to make it more difficult for you to screw up.

Sample Weekly Calendar

TIME	MONDAY
8:00	Math (Text)
8:30	
9:00	English (Conrad, 1/27 notes)
9:30	
10:00	Science (Text, Questions re: lab)
10:30	
11:00	Library (Dante paper) Bring notecards; *finalize topic*
11:30	*beforehand.*
12:00	
12:30	Lunch
1:00	Science lab (Project 3 continuation)
1:30	
2:00	
2:30	
3:00	
3:30	
4:00	Shopping (Mom's B'day present, toothpaaste, soda,
4:30	books for English next week
5:00	
5:30	Meet Cary (at Cindy's)
6:00	
6:30	Dinner
7:00	Math pp. 42-52, problems page 53 (1 hour)
7:30	
8:00	Finish *Heart of Darkness* (3 hours)
9:00	
10:00	
11:00	TV
12:00	Bed

TUESDAY	WEDNESDAY
Math (Text)	History (Quiz)
English (Conrad, 1/27 & 2/1 notes)	
Science (Text, Questions re: lab)	Write up all lab notes; prepare report (talk to Keven re: change of results)
Library —Dante paper—Bring Notecards; Finish initial library research	
Lunch	Lunch
History (Bring Yalta paper; questions re: Roosevelt)	Bookstore: Get Twain bio, *Letters to Earth,* any good commentaries? Work on Twain for next week English
Meet Entrepreneurship Group at Alicia's—list of products/services (6)	
Free time (finish Dante research if necessary)	Movie with Glenn and Marianne; dinner out.
Dinner	
Math pp. 55-71, problems page 72 (1 1/2 hours)	
Prepare for history quiz; review last week's notes; do problems p. 122	History: pp. 123-183 (Recker); pp. 305-359 (Janks)
TV	Think about entrepreneurship project: involvement? time?
Bed	
	Bed

Why are there so many non-study items on this calendar? Study has to be integrated into your life; if you don't list all these other items, you won't be able to correctly allocate study time.

How do you know whether to put an assignment on your weekly calendar or put it on the Project Board first? If it is a simple task *and* if it will definitely be accomplished within a week—read pages 59-78, study for quiz, meet to discuss Cheerleader tryouts with faculty—put it on your weekly calendar. If, however, it's a task that is complicated—requiring further breakdown into specific steps—and/or one that will require more than a week to complete, it should be "flow charted" on your Projects Board. Then the individual steps should be added to your calendar.

Such a detailed calendar is an extreme. And you may not feel you need to include some items. Once your class schedule is in your brain, for example, you may choose to eliminate class listings from your calendar. Or stop listing football practice since it happens every day at the same time. Or leave breaks out because you plan to just take them as needed.

Like anything else, once you have learned to do or use something correctly—exactly as its creator intended you to— you can adapt it to your own needs. So try listing everything on your calendar at the start but then, once you're confident and comfortable in its use, adapting it to fit your specific needs.

But use it!

Using These Tools Effectively

There are thinkers and there are doers.

And there are those who think a lot about doing.

Organizing your life requires you to actually *use* the calendar and Project Board you've constructed, not just waste more time "planning" instead of studying! The primary point to remember is to stick to the rules: Once you have discovered habits and patterns of study that work for you, continue to use and hone them. Be flexible enough to add techniques you learn from others and alter schedules that circumstances have made obsolete, but in the main try to stay on a pre-determined track.

Plan Ahead

Know what you have to do and schedule your work as far ahead as you can manage, but *at least* on a weekly basis. The farther into the future your detailed calendar stretches, the more peace of mind it will give you. You will find it easier to change things around, to know when to be satisfied with just meeting that's week's goals and when to celebrate an unexpected opportunity to move ahead of schedule and lighten the next week's load.

Stay Current

Always keep your calendar up to date, and don't *ever* forget to enter an assignment or appointment! Since your calendar is in a notebook that's always with you, just enter assignments, appointments, notes, etc. as they come up. (While I didn't really tell you you had to carry this calendar with you, if you utilize *your* calendar half as much as *I* do—making it a habit to enter every assignment, every date, every class, every appointment, books to get at the library, things you need to bring along, things to buy, etc.—you'll find quite quickly that having it with you at all times really helps.)

Be Reasonable

Don't try to do too much or too little. Strike a balance, and avoid cramming.

Be Realistic

Plan according to *your* schedule, *your* goals and *your* aptitudes, not some ephemeral "standard." Allocate the time you expect a project to take *you*, not the time it might take someone else, how long your teacher tells you it should take, etc. There will be tasks you accomplish far faster than anyone else, others that take you much longer. Refer back to the original evaluation of your study skills you completed in chapter 1 and take those answers into account as you allocate your study time.

Set Priorities

Try to be realistic and honest with yourself when determining those things which require more effort, those which come easier to you. Refer back to the list of classes you like and dislike or do best and worst in. This will affect the time you need to allocate to specific projects.

Whenever possible, schedule pleasurable activities *after* study time, not before. They will then act as incentives, not distractions.

Be Flexible

No calendar is an island. Any new assignment impacts on whatever you've already scheduled. If you have a reasonably light schedule when a new assignment suddenly appears, it can just be plugged right into your calendar and finished as scheduled. But if you've already scheduled virtually every hour for the next two weeks, *any* addition may force you to change a whole day's plan. Be flexible and be ready. It'll happen.

Monitor And Adjust

No plan of action is foolproof, so monitor your progress at reasonable periods and make changes where necessary. Remember, this is *your* study regimen—you conceived it, you can change it. You may have allocated insufficient time to one assignment, too much to another. Fallen sick, requiring a complete change, gotten a little ahead and decided to run off for a ski weekend, received an unexpected assignment, etc.

I know you'll be anxious to stick to your schedule, to get things done. But taking a break and sitting back to survey the landscape of your efforts provides a good check and balance against costly mistakes and omissions. And don't forget to include the breaks you need, based on your answers in chapter 1, in your allocation of study time.

Follow the Scout Motto

As assignments are entered on your calendar, make sure you also enter items needed—texts, other books you have to buy, borrow or get from the library, special materials (drawing pad, pen and ink, magic markers, graph paper, etc.).

There's nothing worse than sitting down to do that assignment you've put off until the last minute and realizing that though *you're* finally ready to get to work, your supplies *aren't* and that at 10 pm you don't have a lot of options! Make certain you have your study materials available when you need them.

Everything's Relative

Like time. Car trips take longer if you have to schedule frequent stops for gas, food, necessities, etc., longer still if you start one during rush hour. Likewise, libraries are more crowded at certain times of the day or year, which will effect how fast you can get books you need, etc. So take the time of day into account. And if your schedule involves working with others, take *their* sense of time into account—you may find you need to schedule "waiting time" for a chronically-late friend... and make sure you always have a book to read with you.

Try Anything That Works

You may decide that color coding your calendar—red for assignments that must be accomplished that week, blue for steps in longer-term assignments (which give you more flexibility), yellow for personal time and appointments, green for classes, etc.—makes it easier for you to tell at a glance what you need to do and when you need to do it.

Or that you require a day-to-day calendar to carry with you, but also a duplicate one on the wall at home. Once you've gotten used to your class schedule, you may decide to eliminate classes from your calendar and make it less complicated.

Adapt these tools to your own use. Try anything you think may work—use it if does, discard it if it doesn't.

One Thing At A Time

Accomplish one task before going on to the next one—don't skip around. If you ever stuffed envelopes for a political candidate, for example, you've probably already learned that it is far quicker and easier to sign one hundred letters, then stuff them into envelopes, then seal and stamp them than to sign, stuff, seal and stamp one letter at a time.

Do your least favorite chores (study assignments, projects, whatever) first—you'll feel better having gotten them out of the way! And plan how to accomplish them as meticulously as possible—that will get rid of them even faster.

Pizza, Anyone?

If you see that you are moving along faster than you anticipated on one task or project sequence, there's nothing wrong with continuing onto the next part of that assignment or the next project step. The other alternative, of course, is to say *yea!*, forget the next assignment, finish early and buy a pizza.

There's nothing wrong with the latter approach, either.

If you are behind, don't panic. Just take the time to reorganize your schedule and find the time you need to make up. You may be able to free up time from another task, put one part of a long-term project off for a day or two, etc. And if such rescheduling means cancelling a date or missing your favorite TV show, then it's up to you to decide which comes first.

Don't Try To Remember

All of the tools we've discussed and the various other hints, etc. should get you into the habit of writing things down. Amazingly you'll find that not having to remember all these items will free up space in your brain for the things you need to concentrate on or *do* have to remember. As a general rule, write down the so-called little things and you'll avoid data overload and clutter.

But Don't Forget!

As a time management axiom puts it, "Don't respond to the urgent and forget the important." It's easy to become distracted when the phone rings, your baby brother chooses to trash your room or you realize your favorite TV show is coming on. But don't just drop your books and run off. Take a few seconds to make sure you have reached a logical stopping point. If you haven't, get back to work. If you have, jot down a note to yourself of exactly where you left off and/or anything you want to remember after your break. Then you can enjoy your break without anxiety.

Don't Do It Twice

Some assignments—reading a novel, taking notes from a number of library books, etc.—can be interrupted at almost any time without causing a problem. Others may consist of a number of related steps, but you may still be able to pause after any step.

But beware of those time-consuming and complicated tasks which, once begun, demand to be completed. For example, while taking notes from a number of books might be a task you can accomplish in half a dozen sittings, reviewing and organizing all of those notes in order to outline your report requires your undivided attention from start to finish. Interrupting at any point might mean starting all over again. What a waste of time!

If you're writing and suddenly have a brainstorm, just as the phone rings (and you know it's from that person you've been waiting to hear from all week), take a minute to at least jot down your ideas before you stop. Inspiration doesn't always drop in twice the same night. If you let yourself lose your "train of thought," you may find yourself alone at the station, watching your train chug off into the distance.

Someone Always Knows Better

Single out one or two fellow students—preferably ones with better grades—and simply compare notes. Not class notes, *study* notes—find out what's working for somebody else and try to incorporate these techniques into your own program.

Keep Daydreams In Their Place

Nothing can be as counterproductive as losing your concentration, especially at critical times. Learn to ward off those enemies that would alter your course and you will find your journey much smoother.

Interruptions come in two distinct varieties: the unconscious and the conscious. The former include those distractions in your own mind that prevent clear and concentrated thinking—your fantasies and daydreams. Give in to these demons, lose your concentration, and you will find hours happily drifting by. Unfortunately, when you get to the end of the day, you will find you have accomplished nothing on your list. Trust me: the depression from falling behind will not be assuaged by the glow of your fantasies!

One way to guard against these mental intrusions is to know your own study clock and plan your study time accordingly. Each of us is predisposed to function most efficiently at specific times of the day (or night). Find out what sort of study clock you are on and schedule your work during this period. (Most people's peak activity hours fall during the mid-day period. There is a notable reduction of productive hours starting with late afternoon.)

This is not a foolproof solution, however. Even if you've followed your own study profile to a "T," are always on schedule, have every material you need and have organized your calendar with more colors than a box of Crayolas, you may find yourself staring out the window and dreaming of (choose one) a boy, a girl, a night, a weekend, a trip, an adventure, a TV show, a fantasy, or just the way the sun reflects in the pond. Life is like that.

So what do you do?

(1) Banish those thoughts as fast and furiously as Salem handled witches. Shorten the scheduled time before your next break and, when you take that break, enjoy it! Then go back to work. If it continues happening, take more frequent breaks or just keep plugging away. Like anything else, concentration is a learned skill, one in which practice does make perfect.

(2) Say the heck with it and take a break right away. If your schedule is loose enough, give yourself an hour, the morning or even the rest of the day off. Fantasize to your heart's content (or, even better, go out and *do* something about them) and then go back to studying with a mind ready to concentrate on the task at hand.

Neither one of these solutions is always right. There are times to fight the dreams and there are days to say the heck with it and go to a ball game.

Noids To Avoid

The second category of intrusions are conscious acts or activities.

Beware of uninvited guests and *all* phone calls: Unless you are ready to take a break, they will only get you off schedule.

More subtle enemies include the sudden desire to sharpen every pencil in the house, an unheard-of urge to clean your room, an offer to do your sister's homework. Anything, in other words, to avoid your own work. If you find yourself doing anything *but* your work, either take a break then and there or pull yourself together and get down to work. Self-discipline, too, is a learned habit that gets easier with practice.

The simple act of saying "no!" (to others or to yourself) will help insulate yourself from these unnecessary (certainly postponable) interruptions. Remember, what you are seeking to achieve is not just time—but *quality* time. Put your "do not disturb" sign up and stick to your guns, no matter what the temptation.

Reward Yourself

In line with my advice above, there *are* times to ignore the schedule, pat yourself on the back and take off and lay on the grass. But why wait until the siren call of interruption forces you to waste precious time fighting for concentration...especially if you wind up just giving in anyway? Why not incorporate "reward time" into your regular schedule?

Depending on your schedule, of course, this could mean a night off every week to do something you like, a weekend a month, etc. Alternatively, each day (if you really need help, each *hour)* you could simply set up a reward as an incentive for finishing an assignment, a project, a day's work, whatever.

Rewards do not necessarily require large amounts of cash, long trips or other people. The more frequently you run into trouble concentrating on the task at hand, the more frequently you should create some incentive to help yourself: "If I get this next thing done, I'll take off 15 minutes and have an ice cream." Then enjoy the whole banana split!

5

HOW TO
Excel
In
Class

5

Whatever your grade level, whatever your grades, whatever your major, whatever your ultimate career goals, you all have one thing in common: the classroom experience.

Most teachers utilize the classroom setting as an opportunity to embellish and interpret material covered in the text and other assigned readings. If you make certain to cover all your reading assignments and come to class with them as background, then you'll be able to devote your classroom time to the "add-on" angles the teacher will undoubtedly cover.

This chapter will concentrate on how to accomplish key goals within the classroom, specifically how to:

- Get the most out of class lectures
- Participate in a variety of classroom formats
- Take clear and concise notes

Exactly how you use the skills we'll cover in this chapter will be influenced by two key factors: the type of classroom set

up (*Lecture, Discussion Group, Combination* or *Hands-On)*
and, within these formats, the particular methods and styles
employed by each of your teachers.

Listening, Talking Or Doing?

Each of the following general class formats will require
adjustments to accomplish the above goals:

Podium Pleasantries

Teacher speaks, students listen—are quite common
from the college level up, but exist only rarely at the high
school level. Lecture halls at larger colleges may fill up with
hundreds of students for some of the more popular courses (or
those "core" courses required of all entering freshmen). Questions may or may not be asked at some point (primarily by the
students).

Primary Emphasis: Listening; note taking.

Time To Speak Your Mind

Also called tutorials or seminars, discussion groups are
again common on the college level, usually as adjuncts to
courses boasting particularly large enrollments. A typical
weekly schedule for such a course might consist of one lecture
and two discussion groups, two of each or more. Often led by
graduate teaching assistants, these discussion groups are
much smaller—usually no larger than two dozen students,
often 12 - 15—and give students the chance to discuss points
made in the lecture and material from the text and other
assigned reading.

Primary Emphasis: Asking/answering questions; analyzing concepts and ideas; taking part in discussion.

Such groups rarely follow a precise text or format and may wander wildly from topic to topic, once again pointing out the need for a general mastery of the course material, which is the "jumping off" point for discussion.

Most High School...

...and some post-secondary courses are, for want of a better term, *Combination Classes*; that is, they combine the lecture and discussion formats. The teacher prepares a lesson plan of material he or she wants covered in a specific class. Through lecture, question and answer, discussion, audio-visual presentations or a combination of one or more such devices, the material is covered. Your preparation for this type of class will depend to a great extent on the approach of each individual instructor. Such classes also occur on the post-secondary level—college, graduate school, trade school—when class size is small enough to make a formal lecture approach less desirable.

Primary Emphasis: Note taking; listening; participation; asking and answering questions.

Getting Your Hands Dirty

Hands-on classes, including science labs and various vocational education courses (industrial arts, graphics, etc.)— occur at all levels, from high school up. They are concerned almost exclusively with *doing* something—completing a particular experiment, working on a project, etc. The teacher may demonstrate certain things before letting the students work on their own, but the primary emphasis is on the student carrying out his or her own projects while in class. On the college

111

level, science labs are merely overseen by graduate assistants and you're on your own. Trade schools may consist of a combination of short lectures and demonstrations and a series of hands-on workshops—you can't become a good auto mechanic by reading a text or watching someone else clean a distributor.

Primary Emphasis: Development and application of particular manual and technical skills

Rarely can a single class be neatly pigeonholed into one of these formats, though virtually all will be primarily one or another. It would seem that size is a key factor in choosing a format, but you can't always assume, for example, that a large lecture course, filled with 200 or more students, will feature a professor standing behind a rostrum reading from his prepared text. Or that a small class of a dozen people will tend to be all discussion.

During my college years, for example, I had a Religion teacher who, though his class was one of the more popular on campus and regularly drew 300 or more students to each session, rarely lectured at all. In the freewheeling '60s, some professors thought the staid lecture far too *bourgeois* a format for their revolutionary views. So one never knew what to expect when entering his classroom. One week it would be a series of musical improvisations from a local jazz band accompanied by a variety of graduate assistants talking about out-of-body (religious, note the tie-in) experiences. Another session would consist entirely of the professor arguing with a single student over one key topic—one, I might add, that had nothing to do, that *I* could ever fathom, with what we were supposed to be studying that week.

In another class of merely twenty students, the professor teaching us Physical Chemistry would march in at the sound of the bell and, without acknowledging anyone's presence or saying a word, walk to the blackboard and start writing equations, which he would continue to do, working his way across the massive board, until, some twenty or thirty minutes later, he ran off the right side. Slowly, he would walk back to the left side...and start writing all over again. He never asked questions. Never asked *for* questions. In fact, I'm not sure I remember him uttering anything for three solid months!

So though class size should give you some indication of the kind of format that will be employed, there is a lot of room for variation.

Know Your Teacher

What is also extremely important for you to know and understand is the kind of teacher you've got and his or her likes, dislikes, preferences, style and what he or she expects you to get out of his or her class. Depending on your analysis of your teacher's habits, tendencies and goals, preparation may vary quite a bit, whatever the chosen format.

Some teachers are very confident fielding questions at any point during a lesson; others prefer questions to be held until the end of the day's lesson; still others, and my chemistry prof. is a good example, discourage questions (or any interaction for that matter) entirely. Learn when and how your teacher likes to field questions and ask them accordingly.

No matter how ready a class is to enter into a free-wheeling discussion, some teachers fear losing control and veering away from their very specific lesson plan. Such teachers may well encourage discussion but will always try to steer it into the set path they've already decided upon. Other teachers thrive on chaos, in which case you can never be sure just what's going to happen when you walk through the door.

Approaching a class with the former teacher should lead you to participate as much as possible in the class discussion, but warn you to stay within whatever boundaries he or she has obviously set. Getting ready for a class taught by the latter kind of teacher requires much more than just reading the text—there will be a lot of emphasis on your understanding key concepts, interpretation, analysis and your ability to apply those lessons to cases never mentioned in your text at all!

Some teachers' lesson plans or lectures are, at worst, merely a review of what's in the text or, at best, a review plus some discussion of sticky points or areas he or she feels may give you problems. Others use the text or other assignments merely as a jumping off point—their lectures or lesson plans might cover numerous points that aren't in your text at all. Preparing for the latter kind of class will require much more than rote memorization of facts and figures—you'll have to be ready to give examples, explain concepts in context and more.

Most of your teachers and professors will probably have the same goals: to teach you how to think, learn important facts and principles of the specific subject they teach and, perhaps, how to apply them in your own way. But not always: The goal of some teachers will be teaching you to parrot back the facts they deem important, like a social studies teacher who emphasizes your ability to memorize dates or a foreign language teacher who prizes vocabulary lists. In classes like math or science, your ability to apply what you've learned to specific problems is paramount. Others, like your English teacher, will require you to analyze and interpret various works, but may emphasize the "correct" interpretation, too.

Whatever situation you find yourself in—and you may well have one or more of each of the above "types,"—you will need to adapt the skills we will cover in this chapter to each situation.

What To Do Before Class

In general, here's how you should plan to prepare for any class before you walk through the door and take your seat:

Complete All Assignments

Regardless of a particular teacher's style or the classroom format he or she is using, virtually every course you take will have a formal text (or two or three or more) assigned to it. Though the way the text explains or covers particular topics may differ substantially from your teacher's approach to the same material, your text is still the basis of the course and a key ingredient in your studying. You *must* read it, plus any other assigned books, *before* you get to class.

You may sometimes feel you can get away without reading assigned books beforehand, especially in a straight lecture format where you *know* the chance of being called on is slim to none. But fear of being questioned on the material is certainly not the only reason I stress reading the assigned material. You will be lost if the professor decides—for the first time ever! —to spend the entire period asking *you* questions. I've had it happen. And it was *not* a pleasant experience for the unprepared.

You'll also find it harder to take clear and concise notes because you won't know what's in the text, in which case you'll be frantically taking notes on material you'd be underlining in your books, or be able to evaluate important vs. unimportant information.

If you're heading for a discussion group, how can you participate without your reading as a base? I think the lousiest feeling in the world is sitting in a classroom knowing that,

115

sooner or later, you are going to be called on and that you don't know the material.

Remember: This includes not just reading the assigned text but any other books, articles, etc. previously assigned, plus handouts that may have been previously passed out. It also means completing any non-reading assignments—having a paper topic ready, preparing a list of suggested topics, etc.

Review Your Notes

Both from your reading and from the previous class. Your teacher is probably going to start this lecture or discussion from the point he or she left off last time. And you probably won't remember where that point was from week to week... unless you check your notes.

Have Questions Ready

As discussed in chapter 3, preparing questions as you read text material is an important preparatory step. Here's your chance to find the answers to the questions that are still puzzling you. Go over your questions before class. That way, you'll be able to check off the ones the lecturer or teacher answers along the way and only ask those left unanswered.

Prepare Required Materials

Including your notebook, text, pens or pencils and other such basics, plus particular class requirements like a calculator, drawing paper, other books, etc.

Before we get into how to take notes, it's important to talk briefly about how to set up your notebook(s). There are a variety of ways you can organize your note taking system:

1. Get one big two- or- three-ring binder (probably three or more inches thick) that will be used for all notes from all classes. This will require a hole punch, "tab" dividers and a healthy supply of pre-punched paper.

You can divide the binder into separate sections for each course/class, in each of which you will keep notes from your reading, lectures and discussion groups, reading lists, assignment deadlines and any course handouts, all material set up in chronological fashion. Alternatively, you can further subdivide each section into separate sections for reading notes, class notes and handouts.

2. Use one of the above systems but get smaller binders, one for each course/class.

3. Use separate notebooks (they're a lot lighter than binders) for notes, both from your reading and class. Use file folders for each class to keep handouts, project notes and copies, etc. They can be kept in an accordion file or in a multi-pocketed folder.

Whichever system you choose—one of the above or an ingenious one of your own—do *not* use the note card system for preparing papers and oral reports you will learn in chapter 7. While it's my all-time favorite system for that application, it does *not* work well for class note taking...and I've tried it.

What To Do In Class

Keep in mind your own preferences and under what circumstances you do best—refer back to the first two chapters and review your skills lists. You'll need to concentrate hardest on those courses in which you do most poorly, no matter what the style of the teacher.

You'll also want to make sure you're sitting where you prefer (near a door or window, near the front or back of the classroom, etc.).

And don't discount the importance of the way you approach each class mentally—getting the most out of school in general and any class in particular depends in good measure on how ready you are to really take part in the process. You must be "up" for school, "up" for each class. It is *not* sufficient, even if you're otherwise well-prepared, to just sit back and absorb the information. Learning requires your active participation every step of the way.

Taking Notes

Taking concise, clear notes is first and foremost the practice of discrimination—developing your ability to separate the essential from the superfluous, the key concepts, key facts, key ideas from all the rest. In turn, this requires the ability to listen to what you're teacher is saying and copying down only what you need to in order to understand the concept. For some, that could mean a single sentence. For others, a detailed example will be the key. Just remember: The quality of your notes usually has little to do with their length—three key lines that reveal the core concepts of a whole lecture are far more valuable than paragraphs of less important data.

To listen and effectively separate the wheat from the chaff in a lecture or lesson is difficult to do if you must laboriously write out even the simplest notes. Learn to take shorthand—either an established system or your own makeshift one of abbreviations and symbols. This will allow you to concentrate more on the teacher and less on your notebook.

Do not, as some college students prefer, tape record your professor's lectures. It will take you twice or thrice as long to transcribe the tape as to listen to the lecture in the first place.

Let's look at an example—a passage from a book I just finished editing, <u>Your First Book of Wealth</u> by A. David Silver —to illustrate the kind of selective note taking I'm emphasizing. With minor variations, this passage could be delivered as a lesson by a high school instructor teaching an entrepreneurship course or incorporated into a college professor's lecture on "Business basics for the non-Business major":

W = P x S x E, where W = Wealth; P = the size of the Problem that the entrepreneur has identified; S = the elegance of the entrepreneur's Solution. In the case of a product, this is a combination of its proprietary nature and its appropriateness to the market. In terms of a service, the uniqueness of the marketing systems is the biggest factor.; and E = the quality of the Entrepreneurial team—the experience, competence and degree of cooperation of and between the members of the company's initial management group.

In other words, the amount of wealth created is determined by multiplying the size of the problem, the elegance (uniqueness and effectiveness) of the solution and the competence of the people executing the solution.

There are two important things to notice about any such equation. The greater the values of P, S and E— the bigger the problem, better the solution, more competent the team—the greater amount of wealth (W) created in the shortest period of time. On the other hand, any time any *one* of those three values (P, S or E) is zero, so is W—because multiplying any number, no matter *how* large, by zero still equals zero.

In the mid-1970s, John Z. DeLorean created a solution—the DeLorean automobile—that was not unique and did not have a non-duplicable delivery system. Thus, the "S" factor of DeLorean Motor Co. was zero. What's more, it was a solution for a problem that didn't exist—there were already many sports cars in the marketplace. So the "P" factor was also zero. Multiplying any value of "E" by one zero would already give a zero value for "W." Two zeros didn't make it any worse, but certainly didn't change the outcome. As a result, the investors in DeLorean Motor Co. lost their money—nearly $125 million—in a very short period of time and DeLorean found himself spending the next three years in court (where he was acquitted of both fraud and narcotics charges).

On the other hand, Intel Corp. produced a large amount of wealth for its entrepreneurial team (Robert L. Noyce, Andrew Grove and Gordon Moore) in less than ten years. In 1968, they identified the Problem: The high cost and large size of core memory used in mainframe computers made such large computers useful to a very small number of people. Their solution was the development of metal oxide semiconductor memories placed on silicon chips, which reduced both the cost and size of core memory. The Intel founders— the Entrepreneurial team—had worked together in similar positions at Fairchild Semiconductor Corp. and knew what they were doing. The entrepreneurs and their principal backer, Arthur Rock, invested approximately $2 million in Intel in 1968. Ten years later, the company's valuation (W) in the stock market was nearly $2 billion. Not incidentally, Intel's solution turned out to be the key to the development of personal computers, arguably the most important and far-reaching technological development of the last two decades.

Here's the way *my* notes would look if this information was delivered in a lecture and had not previously been covered in any assigned text:

1. W = PxSxE (P=Sz/Prbl; S=Elg(Unq)/Sol; E=Cmptnce/E Tm)

2. XM 1: DeLorean. S=0, P=0. Failed—invst lst all.

3. XM2: Intel—Sucfl. Big P-sz&cst comp mem=min use. S=mtl oxd smicond mems. Strt 1968 w/ $2mil v.c. W=2 bil. S base 4 pers comp.

What? You have no idea what these notes mean? You're not supposed to—I've used my own shorthand. Here's the way I would "translate" my notes when I was ready to review (with the key words I abbreviated underlined to show how my system works):

$W = P \times S \times E$, where P = the size of the problem; S = the elegance (uniqueness) of the solution; and E = the competence of the entrepreneurial team.

The first example ("XM 1")—the DeLorean motor car, in which both S and P were zero (i.e., problem was not one crying for solution—many cars exist—and solution was not particularly unique). So $W = 0$ ("failed"), meaning, as expected, investors lost whatever capital they had put up.

Second example ("XM 2")—Intel—was successful. They had identified a big problem—the size and cost of the memories of large computers meant few people ("minimum") could make use of them. Intel's solution was the creation of metal oxide semiconductor memories, which reduced both size and cost. Started in 1968 with $2 million from a venture capitalist, Intel is now worth ("W" = Wealth) $2 billion. And its solution was the basis for the development of the personal computer.

Now, I actually called this a system. It really isn't, since, unlike standard shorthand systems, I change abbreviations all the time—entrepreneurial was just "E" in these notes because I would be able to figure out the context and realize that's what *I* meant by "E," and not Excellence, Entropy or any other word starting with "E." In some other lecture where the subject itself wasn't "Entrepreneurship," I wouldn't try to get a single "E" to stand for the word!

The point, though, is my "system" works for me and, it should be obvious, enables me to take very few notes and really concentrate on the instructor. And it doesn't matter if your notes make sense to anyone but you; they're not supposed to. Just make sure *you* can make sense out of them!

Leaving the shorthand aside, notice that numerous facts —the names of Intel's founders, how much DeLorean's investors lost, etc.—were completely (and purposely) left out of my notes. Why? I simply concluded that the formula was the key to the whole lecture and all I needed to write down were the key points made by the two examples to make sure I understood how the formula could be applied to any entrepreneurial endeavor.

Participating

In many non-lecture classes, you will find that discussion, mostly in the form of questions and answers, is actively encouraged. This dialogue serves to both confirm your knowledge and comprehension of specific subject matter and identify those areas in which you need work.

Whatever the format in which you find yourself, participate in any discussion to the best of your ability. Most teachers consider class participation a key ingredient in the grades they mete out. No matter how many papers and tests you ace, if you never open your mouth in class, you may be surprised (but shouldn't be) to get less than an "A."

If you are having trouble following a particular line of thought or argument, ask for a review or for clarification.

Don't ask questions or make points looking to impress your teacher—your real motive will probably be pretty obvious. Remember what you're there for—to learn the material and master it.

Based on the professor's preferences and the class set up, ask the questions you feel need answers.

Finally, listen closely to the words of your classmates. Knowledge has no boundaries and you'll often find their comments, attitudes and opinions as helpful and insightful as your instructor's.

What if you're shy or just get numb whenever you're called on? Ask a question rather than taking part in the discussion—it's easier and, over time, may help you break the ice and jump into the discussion. If you really can't open your mouth without running a fever, consider a remedial course, like Dale Carnegie.

Most importantly, prepare and practice. Fear of standing in front of a class or even of participating from the safety of your seat is, for many of you, really a symptom of lack of confidence. And *lack of confidence stems from lack of preparation.* The more prepared you are—if you know the material backwards and forwards—the more likely you will be able, even *want,* to raise your hand and strut your stuff.

Practicing with friends, parents or relatives—even to standing in front of a group of friends and trying to get over the "sweats" that inevitably occur—may also help.

If you are having trouble with oral reports, they are covered separately in chapter 7. I think you'll find the hints I've included there will eliminate a lot of the fear such talks seem to engender.

What To Do After Class

As soon as possible after your class, review your notes, fill in the "blanks," mark down questions you need to research in your text or ask during the next class, and remember to mark any new assignments on your weekly calendar.

I tend to discourage recopying your notes as a general practice, since I believe it's more important to work on taking good notes the first time around and not wasting the time it takes to recopy. *But* if you tend to write fast and illegibly, it might also be a good time to rewrite your notes so they're readable, taking the opportunity to summarize as you go. Remember, the purpose of your note taking is to have a complete data base to follow and re-reference at some later date. The better your notes, the better your chance of capturing and recalling the pertinent material.

It is not easy for most high school students to do so, but in college, where you have a greater say in scheduling your classes, this is why I recommend "one period on, one off"—an open period, even a half hour, after each class, to review that class's notes and prepare for the next one.

6

HOW TO

Use Your Library

6

Libraries contain the written record of Humankind's brief stay on Planet Earth. They stand unparalleled as one of our finest accomplishments and unchallenged as a reference and research source. In your attempt to develop lifelong study skills, you will find yourself using this resource constantly. The library presents to us a single well from which we can draw knowledge and material throughout our lifetimes... without ever worrying about coming up dry.

Libraries are a staple in cities large and small throughout the land and represent an amazingly democratic aspect of our culture. Rules and restrictions vary from library to library —public vs. college, large vs. small, etc.—but high school and college students usually have access to virtually all library materials. And remember: These services are *free*. A library card lets you borrow as many books as you want (though there are some limits on how many you can have at one time). It's your ticket to the world of knowledge that could keep you busy for the rest of your life.

Where To Find A Library

Start with your local phone directory. I can virtually guarantee there is a library within minutes of your home, since according to the two volumes of the 41st edition of *The American Library Directory* (R. R. Bowker, New York, NY), there are 15,013 public and 4,647 academic (high school, college, university and graduate school) libraries in the United States. These are the ones you would most likely be using. (Naturally, you'll find these volumes, with listings of all U. S. libraries by state and city, in your library. I've listed names, addresses and collection statistics for ten major metropolitan public libraries in the U. S. later in this chapter.)

If for some reason you don't think the resources of these nearly 20,000 libraries are sufficient, there are also 488 libraries on military bases throughout the country, plus 1,687 government and 9,860 special (law, medical, religious, art, etc.) libraries nationwide.

Many major university libraries dwarf all but the largest public library systems. Harvard, at over 8,000,000 volumes the largest university library in the country, Yale, Princeton, the University of Illinois at Urbana-Champaign and other such bastions of learning offer tremendous resources even the major public libraries can't. If you have access to a college or university library, consider it your good fortune and take advantage of it.

How Libraries Work

Most libraries are divided into reading rooms, unrestricted book stacks and restricted collections. Unrestricted book stacks are those through which anyone using the library can wander, choosing books to use while in the library or, if allowed, to take home. Restricted areas generally include any special collections of rare books, those open only to scholars or to those with particular credentials, either by library rule or by order of whoever donated the collection (and, often, the room housing it) to the library. In some libraries, *all* book stacks are closed, and *all* books must be obtained from a librarian.

Most libraries contain both *circulating materials*—those books and other items you may check out and take home with you—and *non-circulating material*—those that must be used only in the library. All fiction, general nonfiction and even most "scholarly" titles will usually be found in the first group. Reference material, periodicals and books in special collections are usually in the second.

How To Use Your Library

So as to provide organization and facilitate access, most libraries utilize the Dewey Decimal Classification System, which uses numbers from 000 to 999 to break down all material by subject matter. It begins by organizing all books into ten major groupings:

000 - 099	General
100 - 199	Philosophy
200 - 299	Religion
300 - 399	Social Sciences
400 - 499	Philosophy
500 - 599	Science
600 - 699	Useful Arts
700 - 799	Fine Arts
800 - 899	Literature
900 - 999	History

Given the millions of books available in major libraries, just dividing them into these ten groups would still make it quite difficult to find a specific title. So each of the ten major groupings is further divided into ten and each of these now one hundred groups is assigned to more specific subjects within each large group. For example, within the Philosophy classification (100), 150 is psychology and 170 is ethics. Within the history classification (900), 910 is travel and 930 is ancient history.

There is even further subdivision. Mathematics falls within the Science classification (500) and is given its own number in the 500 series—510. But specific subjects within mathematics are further classified: 511 is arithmetic; 512, algebra, and so on.

Finally, to simplify your task even more, the last two digits in the Dewey code signify the type of book:

01	Philosophy of
02	Outlines of
03	Dictionary of
04	Essays about
05	Periodicals on
06	Society transactions and proceedings
07	Study of or teaching of
08	Collections
09	History of

There are more than 50,000 new books published each year, and your library probably buys a great number of these. Books arrive almost daily and are sent to the cataloguing section for classification, special bindings (if needed) and shelf placement. Once entered into the system, books are indexed in the card catalogue by author, title and subject matter. Finding a biography of Tolstoy, for example, is as easy as looking up

Tolstoy in the card catalogue and copying down the appropriate codes for the particular one you want (yes, your library probably has more than one!).

In a closed-shelf environment, you would give the appropriate numbers to a librarian and the books would be delivered to you. If the shelves are open, you have merely to learn the way they are organized and go search after your own books. Open shelf areas are often designated by letters of the alphabet (for fiction), by subject matter (in smaller libraries), or, in virtually all major libraries, according to the Dewey classification code.

You may go to your local library and not even find a card catalogue, which might confuse you. Am I out of touch? Hopelessly antiquated? Computers are taking over the world of business, so it's no surprise that a record-intensive "business" like the library is in the forefront of computerization. Librarians I've spoken to estimate that by the year 2000—just a little more than a decade from now—95% of all U. S. libraries will be "on line"—with "user friendly" computer terminals replacing old fashioned catalog cards. Roughly 30% of all libraries—maybe yours—already *are* on line.

Computers also mean more things you can do. For example, at the New York Public Library there are Apple microcomputers offering more than 100 programs, from practice math problems to SAT preparation and, of course, computer games, at more than 30 locations, .

A Look At A Major Library

How extensive is the collection of information at a major institution like the New York Public Library?

You'd be amazed.

Let's look only at the main library on Fifth Avenue, which stands like a monument at the dividing line between the East and West sides of Manhattan.

The first thing you discover is that no books can be taken out of this building. There are 81 branches throughout the five boroughs of New York that *will* let you take out many of their holdings, so this is not a problem.

So you can't take anything with you. What can you study while you're there? In addition to an extensive collection of the fiction and non-fiction works you'd expect to find in such a library, shelves of books on every conceivable topic from Airplanes to Zoology, back issues of more periodicals than you could probably name and more recordings than your local record store stocks, there are separate rooms—that's right, *rooms* (and large ones, too!)—for prints and photographs, art, microfilm, U.S. and local history and genealogy, rare books, manuscripts, archives, maps, a Science and Technology Research Center, Economic and Public Affairs Center, Slavonic and Oriental Divisions. (In the system as a whole there's also an extensive Afro-American collection and a separate Library for the Blind and Physically Handicapped.) While a few of the more specialized collections (rare books, manuscripts, prints and photographs) require a special card just to enter the collection, most of the rest of this amazing storehouse of knowledge is open to the public!

But the NYPL also demonstrates through its many programs that the library is much more than just a repository for books. It offers a daily program of films, lectures, book discussion groups, plays, poetry readings, concerts and exhibits for adults, films, story telling and pre-school programs for children, and is a meeting place for a wide variety of community, consumer, educational, health, social service, religious, cultural and recreational groups.

You could live at the NYPL and *never* get bored!

What About *Your* Library?

What? You don't live in New York? And you doubt your local library can compete?

You'd be surprised at how wrong you probably are. I live in Hawthorne, N. J., a small suburban community. My local library—the Louis Bay IInd Library, officially—is probably typical of the kind of library you'll be working in. So a look at my library should help you appreciate what you can do at yours.

According to Bill Breedlove, library director, its collection included (as of 2/1/89) 66,000 books, current and back issues of 166 magazines and newspapers, plus a variety of other material: microfiche, microfilm, compact discs, audio cassettes, phonograph records, videotapes, plus children's books and audio tapes, filmstrips and videocassettes. Not unimpressive, but a mere one hundredth of the collection available at the NYPL.

Ah, but remember the wonders the computer hath wrought. Through a worksharing program with the library of Fairlawn, the community next door, you can sit in the Hawthorne library and search on-line through Fairlawn's collection of books—another 150,000 volumes. And if you need other periodicals, you have computer access to a list of the 1,500 titles in the nearby Fairleigh Dickinson University library, any of which you can obtain in less than a day. (Within a year, material will be FAXed in minutes.)

By the end of 1989, you could sit at a computer terminal in Hawthorne and access the more than 6,000,000 volumes at Princeton University's Firestone Library, the second largest library in the New York Metropolitan area (after the New York Public Library) and larger than any other public library in the nation (except for the gargantuan Library of Congress, which is a special case).

Right now, by networking with other libraries, my Hawthorne librarian could track down virtually any book, magazine, newspaper, phonograph record, audio or video cassette you want if given a reasonable amount of time. And networking is the word of the future. In New Jersey, for example, many of the counties have already tied together all the individual libraries within their borders. In two to three years, every county in New Jersey will have a county-wide library networking system in place. One to two years after that, every library in the *state* will be tied together by connecting all the county systems. Don't be surprised if within our lifetimes— and I left Teenland some years ago—even the smallest libraries will boast computer terminals that will enable you to call up any book or periodical in any other library...in the world.

Where To Start

Each of us who has become familiar with the wonders of the library has probably developed our own approach to enjoying them and using them most efficiently. My own experience emphasizes what may be the obvious: Getting the right start is all important. Since I try to keep from being overwhelmed with material, I start any research working with the broadest outlines or topics (and the broadest resources) and wind my way down the ladder, getting more and more specific in topic and sources as I go.

Let's assume, for example, that you have to prepare a report on the latest attempts to combat apartheid and fit this effort into a historical perspective. Here's how you might approach the task:

1. Go to a dictionary and look up the term apartheid. Make certain you have a firm understanding of what this word means before you proceed any further!

2. Consult any one of the numerous leading encyclopedias you will find in your library—Britannica, Americana, Collier's, The World Book, etc. Here you will find an overview and historical prospective on the subject of these special racial laws. Encyclopedic entries are usually the most comprehensive and concise you will find. Since they cover so much territory and are continually being updated and revised, they are an ideal "big-picture" resource.

3. With overview in hand, you can start consulting the major indexes and directories your library has to develop a list of more specific resources:

The New York Times Index will give you a complete listing of news articles pertaining to the matter that have appeared in the "Newspaper of Record."

The Readers Guide to Periodical Literature will list articles that have appeared in every major magazine.

The Book Review Digest lists all current book titles with a digest of each one's contents.

Just by consulting these general references—and without yet consulting any of the specific resources to which they will lead you —you would already have accomplished a great deal. At the very least, you will already know something about apartheid in general, its history and many related areas.

Obviously, the entries in these major resources can then be directly consulted—specific *New York Times* issues on microfilm, periodicals at the periodicals desk, etc. And, of course, your card catalogue or computer terminal will spew out listings for hundreds of other books on the general issue of apartheid or any related subject it touches (which you learned about through your skimming of the above general resources) —The African National Congress, Nelson and Winnie Mandela, Prime Minister Botha, black homelands, Archbishop Desmond Tutu, etc.

In one brief tour of your library's resources, you'll easily discover and know how to obtain more material than you would need to write a book on apartheid, let alone a report.

What if you're uncomfortable in the library? Or an infrequent user? Or simply find it a confusing place that's more trouble than it's worth? As we've been saying all along, developing any habit is just a matter of practice. The more you use the library, the more comfortable you will become using it. And, of course, the more books you will become familiar with. In a very short time, you will have your own "personal" list of resources that you start with whenever you receive an assignment—a favorite encyclopedia, directory, index, etc.

If you want the library to become like a second home, its every shelf a familiar friend, why not go to work there? Many libraries—smaller ones in particular—offer opportunities for paid and volunteer work. Even if you work for free, this is an excellent way to learn the ins and outs of your library. Many of you might not use the library as much as you should or even would like because it's just a confusing series of catacombs. The more comfortable you are—the more you know about where materials are—the more you will want to use it. And the more help you will be able to obtain from this great resource that's just waiting to welcome you!

Major Metropolitan Library Systems

For those of you living in or near major U.S. cities, I've listed the names, addresses, phone numbers and number of volumes for the major public libraries in them. Note that most of these are public facilities, so access to them is at no charge. The entry for "Holdings" is the total number of volumes in each library. The number of branches follows each listing (in parentheses)

New York Public Library (81)
5th Avenue at 42nd Street
New York, New York 10018
(212) 930-0800
Library Holdings: 6,500,000

Los Angeles Public Library (62)
630 W. Fifth Street
Los Angeles, CA 90071-2097
(213) 612-3200
Holdings: 5,663,000

Free Library of Philadelphia (48)
Logan Square
Philadelphia, PA 19103-1157
(215) 686-5822
Holdings: 4,633,041

Chicago Public Library
425 N. Michigan Avenue
Chicago, Illinois 60611
(312) 269-2900
Holdings: 4,764,673

Boston Public Library (26)
Copley Square
Boston, MA 12117-0286
(617) 536-5400
Holdings: 5,806,895

Library of Congress
Independence Avenue at First St. E.
Washington, D.C. 20546
(203) 282-5000
Holdings: 22,518,081**

**Publishers are required by copyright law to deposit copies of each book they publish with the Library of Congress.

Dallas Public Library (19)
1515 Young Street
Dallas, Texas 75201-9987
(214) 670-1400
Holdings: 2,296,310

Miami Dade Public Library
System (28)
101 West Flagler Street
Miami, Florida 33180-1523
(305) 375-2665
Holdings: 2,386,204

St. Louis County Library (16)
1640 S. Lindbergh Blvd.
St. Louis, Mo. 63131-3598
(314) 994-3300
Holdings: 2,125,315

San Francisco Public Library
Civic Center
San Francisco, CA 94102
(415) 558-4235
Holdings: 594,551

Exercises

1. Complete details of President Kennedy's assassination can be found in: (a) New York Times Index (b) Encyclopedia Brittanica (c) Book Review Digest

2. To research a paper on great art figures of the 20th Century, I would be best advised to consult: (a) College library (b) Public Library (c) Metropolitan Museum of Art

3. The main entry card for most books classified by the Dewey Decimal System is usually the: (a) Author card (b) Title card (c) Subject card

4. The primary characteristic of an encyclopedia is that it is: (a) Multi-volumal (b) Frequently updated (c) Comprehensive with regard to subject matter

5. Libraries frequently do the following with respect to books most in demand: (a) Charge a lending fee (b) Put them on reserve (c) Lend them for an unlimited time period

6. Most libraries receive their funding from: (a) The government (b) Private sources (c) A combination of a & b.

7. The following are usually available at major libraries: (a) Microfilm files (b) Current newspapers and magazines (c) Paperback best sellers

8. Encyclopedias provide a good overview of: (a) An entire subject (b) Individual sections of a broad topic (c) Material which can be utilized as a starting point for more detailed research

9. Most libraries have a: (a) Reading room (b) TV room (c) Discussion room

To determine your "library literary rating," check the answers on page 183.

7

HOW TO
Write Better Papers

7

Whatever your grade level, whatever your major, sooner or later you'll have to prepare written and/or oral reports for virtually every one of your classes. If you're like most students, your reaction will be the same every time: "Oh, no, why me? What do I do now? Where do I start?"

I'm not going to pretend that reading this chapter will make you such a good writer that you can quit school and start visiting bookstores to preen in front of the window displays featuring your latest best seller.

But there is absolutely no reason to fear a paper or oral report. Once you know the simple steps to take and rules to follow to complete it satisfactorily.

Once you realize that 90% of preparing a paper has *nothing* to do with writing or even being able to write. And once you're confident that preparing papers accord-ing to my suggestions will probably get you a grade or two higher than you've gotten before...even if you are the world's poorest excuse for a writer.

The Five Basic Rules

Let's start with the basic rules that need to be emblazoned on your wall:

1. *Always* follow your teacher's directions to the letter.
2. *Always* hand in your paper on time.
3. *Always* hand in a clean and clear copy of your paper.
4. *Never* allow a spelling or grammatical error in your papers.
5. *Always* keep at least one copy of every paper you write.

Follow Directions

Your teacher's directions may include:

• A general subject area from which topics should be chosen—"some aspect of Roosevelt's presidency," "a 19th century invention," "a short story by Edgar Allan Poe," etc.

• Specific requirements regarding format—typed, double-spaced, include title page, don't include title page, etc.

• Suggested length—e.g., 10-15 typewritten pages.

• Other requirements—turn in general outline before topic is approved; get verbal OK on topic before proceeding; don't include quotes (from other works) longer than a single paragraph; and any other idiosyncrasies of your own teachers.

Whatever his or her directions, **follow them *to the letter*.** High school teachers may be somewhat forgiving, but I have known college professors to simply refuse to accept a paper that was not prepared as they instructed—and gave the poor but wiser student an "F" for it.

If you are unsure of a specific requirement or if the suggested area of topics is unclear, it is *your* responsibility to talk to your teacher and clarify whatever points are confusing you. It is not a bad idea to prepare two or three topics you'd like to write about and seek his or her preliminary approval if the assignment seems particularly vague.

Be On Time

Since you've studied and memorized chapter 4, there is certainly no reason, short of catastrophic illness or life-threatening emergency, for you to *ever* be late with an assignment. Barring those, there is rarely an acceptable excuse for being late. Again, some teachers will refuse to accept a paper that is late. At best, they will do so but mark you down for your lateness, perhaps turning an "A" paper into a "B" or worse.

Appearance Counts

Teachers have to read a lot of papers and shouldn't be faulted for being human if, after hundreds of pages, they come upon your jelly-stained, pencil-written tome and get a bit discouraged. Nor should you be surprised if they give you a lower grade than the content might merit just because the presentation is so poor.

I am not advocating "form over substance." Far from it —the content is what the teacher is looking for, and he or she will primarily be basing your grade on *what* you write. But presentation is important. So follow these simple rules:

• If you must handwrite a paper, use a pen, not a pencil.

• If your handwriting is atrocious, *don't* handwrite your papers.

143

• If you type (or have someone type) your paper, use clean white bond and (preferably) a new carbon ribbon so that the images are crisp and clear.

• Unless otherwise instructed, always double space a typewritten paper.

• Use a simple typeface that is clear and easy-to-read; avoid those that are too big—stretching out a five-page paper into ten—or too small (and hard to read).

• And never use a fancy italic, modern or otherwise ornate or hard to read typeface for the entire paper.

Learn To Spel Gud

Serious and constant spelling and grammatical errors do not just count in English class—virtually every teacher or professor I've ever had showed at least a passing awareness of grammar, spelling, sentence structure, etc. and took it into consideration when grading my papers.

If you are a terrible speller and a worse grammarian, I would strongly suggest a remedial course. These areas will not miraculously improve now that you're beyond the elementary grades where you were *supposed* to learn these basic skills. And these are skills that you will be required to utilize far beyond your school years, after which the penalty for your inability to do so may well be disheartening: I throw away *any* resume I receive from a prospective job or internship applicant in which there is *one* spelling error. That includes their cover letters, too. And I don't think I'm harder than any other prospective employer out there.

Get very familiar with a good dictionary and a basic grammar book, like Strunk & White's The Elements of Style. Read the latter, keep both on your desk and use them as often as necessary. Something like the Chicago Manual of Style,

New York Times Style Book or Associated Press Style Book can also be extremely helpful in setting up a system you can consistently follow.

Lastly, find someone who is better than you are at these skills—parent, relative, friend—and ask *them* to proofread your papers before you hand them in.

Ten Cents A Page...

... Is the most it costs these days to photocopy your paper; carbon paper is even cheaper. Whichever method you use, always keep a copy of every paper you write. Teachers and professors have been known to lose things.

I would also suggest you keep your notes and drafts of each paper in a separate file folder at home. It is not that unusual for a professor to question someone's sources, even the originality of their ideas; it is helpful if you have your original research to back up your authorship of a paper or report. You may also find these notes helpful on other projects now and in the future.

The Sixth And Seventh Rules

These get plastered on your wall and *underlined:*

• Complete any assignment to the best of your ability.

• Remember that the purpose of any paper is to communicate facts, thoughts and interpretations, not to impress with length, verbiage or the size of your thesaurus.

How to do *that* is what the rest of this chapter is about.

The Fry Paper-Writing System

As you already learned in chapter 4, the more complex a task or the longer you need to complete it, the more important your organization becomes. By breaking down any paper-writing project into a series of manageable steps, you'll start to feel less chaotic, hectic and scared right away.

Here are the steps that, with some minor variations along the way, are common to virtually any written report or paper:

1) Finalize topic
2) Carry out initial library research
3) Prepare general outline
4) Do detailed library research
5) Prepare detailed outline (from note cards)
6) Write first draft
7) Do additional research (if necessary)
8) Write second draft
9) Spell check and proofread
10) Have someone else proofread
11) Produce final draft
12) Proofread

Choosing A Topic

As mentioned previously, the absolute first step is to decide on the topic you intend to write about, presuming it isn't simply assigned. This step, however, also includes understanding that topic and summarizing it in such a way that encourages you to choose a specific direction for your research.

Do *not* feel you have to choose a topic without any help. I strongly urge you to do some initial library research, perhaps on two or three potential topics, and *then* choose one. This will help you clearly define your topic and get a better handle on its direction right from the start. And reversing steps one and two also means you will have a better idea of the materials—and the extent of them—before you choose a topic. There's nothing wrong with choosing a topic on which a lot of information is available and avoiding one that no one seems to have written about since 1927.

Initial Library Research

This requires using the general references—encyclopedias, bibliographic indexes, periodical indexes, etc.—we discussed in chapter 6. These (especially encyclopedias) are *not* the key sources to consult to write your paper—most teachers I've known are intimately familiar with the major reference works in the local library and frown on a simple rehash of the information from an article in one of them. They are, however, an excellent place to start your search for the *primary* ("I was there and here's what happened") and *secondary* ("I wasn't there but I read the accounts of everybody who was and here's what they said") resources that will form your reading list.

Remember, this is an investigative process in which you are mining the library's volumes to determine what is available. After you have gathered the material, you will then add your own interpretation to it. At this opening juncture, you are only on a fact-finding mission.

What you should attempt to know/have when you have completed this step:

• A basic understanding of the general topic you're writing about

• At least a notion of a more specific topic and/or a particular point of view

• A list of primary and secondary resources to consult

• Short and concise notes on the "general headings" that will appear in your paper, from which you can construct your general outline.

Two important points:

1) Don't be afraid to settle on a topic but modify or even change it as your research develops. If you've discovered a unique point of view or a relatively unexplored area that interests you, be prepared to adapt as you go. The more interested you are in the paper you're writing, the better job you will do.

And 2) List all of the primary and secondary sources you intend to consult on separate 3 x 5 note cards (I prefer the lined ones). They are available at any stationery and most drug stores.

Number each card in the upper left (1, 2, 3). *Don't* use letters—what do you do if you actually use more than 26 books? Start on the Chinese alphabet? On each card, write the title of *one* book, its author and its library classification number. You can, if you wish, write a short note to yourself on the bottom or back about exactly where it's located if you've found it but are afraid you won't remember where!

This is the beginning of your 3 x 5 card system, a simple but highly effective research tool I'll be discussing in much more detail a little later in this chapter.

The General Outline

Your general outline can be remarkably short and sweet. How could it be much more? You've barely learned enough to do it, let alone add details. Remember: The general outline is merely an attempt to write down the topics you will be covering and the order in which you will write about them. For example, let's presume you have been assigned a major (25 pages!) paper: "Can The U. S. Trade Deficit Be Reversed?"

Your general outline might look like this (and use letters rather than numbers. You'll see why a little later):

A. Definition and explanation of causes

B. History of trade deficits

C. Political effects

D. Special legislative/monetary programs

E. Current economic opinions (leaders)

F. Implications (include potential countermeasures)

That's all—just the "bare bones" to which your detailed library research will add flesh.

Detailed Library Research

Remember the 3 x 5 cards on which you wrote the materials you wanted to consult? Take them out and start finding those books and articles!

Using your general outline as a guide, check the table of contents and index of the first book on your list. If it has information on any of the topics your paper will focus on, it's time to sit down and start taking notes.

First, write all of the additional bibliographic data on the 3 x 5 card on which you wrote the title, author and library number. This should include the edition (if none is listed on the front or back of the title page, assume it's the first) and/or volume number, number of pages, place and date of publication. You will need this information if you plan to include a bibliography or list of references at the end of your paper,

What if the book has nothing helpful for you? Throw the card away. Don't worry about there being a missing number. It doesn't matter.

Magazine articles, newspaper articles, video or audio cassettes—whatever source you're consulting, write down all of the appropriate data you'll need for your bibliography on separate note cards.

Now, here's where the 3 x 5 card system really comes to the fore. Let's presume the book on Card #1 has a lot of material and you're ready to sit down and take some serious notes. You're also going to use 3 x 5 cards to take all your notes, according to the following strict (i.e., you *must* follow them with *no* exceptions) rules:

• One *and only one* thought, idea, quote or fact is to be written on each card.

• Quotes should never be carried over to another card (if they are, they're too long). You can, however, write on the back of note cards.

• Write the number assigned to the resource (in this case, "1") in the upper left-hand corner of the card.

• Write the page number on which the material you're taking notes appears on the first line, far left (e.g., "34)").

• In the upper right-hand corner, put the letter of the sub-topic to which this note applies. (There will occasionally be quotes, facts, figures, opinions, etc. which you feel are important but can't immediately fit into one of the major sub-topics of your general outline. Consider assigning another letter—in this case, "G," the first unused one—for these miscellaneous notes. You'll try to fit them into your paper after you've completed a more detailed outline.)

• Write a *very* brief—one or two words if possible—note following the letter on the specific information contained on the card.

Continue taking notes from all of the resources your initial library research unearthed. And don't be afraid to add others you discover along the way—just make sure you make a bibliographic card for each resource you use, even if you take only one note from it, and faithfully follow the above rules.

When you have completed your library research, you will have a stack of 3 x 5 cards in no particular order—100, 300, maybe more. It's time to move to the next step.

Detailed Outline

Your detailed outline is already complete.

Wait a minute. You've just gotten home from the library and haven't even *started* writing a detailed outline. How could it be done?

Remember the letters you wrote in the upper right-hand corner of each card? They are your key to easily organizing your notes. Take each card and make seven separate stacks (order within each stack doesn't matter), one for each letter of your general outline and one stack of miscellaneous cards. You've now organized your notes by sub-topics.

Go to stack "A" and go through the brief notes following the letter "A" in the upper right-hand corner. Let's presume there are only three such notes that appear on one or more of the cards—"Definition," "Cause—Overvalued Currency" and "Cause—Excess Demand." You now know what details you intend to include in the first part of your paper. Group the cards according to the topic they cover and, if you wish, start writing your detailed outline based on your notes.

After doing this for each stack of cards ("A" through "F"), you might wind up with an outline that looks something like this:

Outline—U.S. Trade Deficit Paper

1. Introduction
   A. Definition of deficit and trade deficit
   B. What's caused it?
      1. Overvalued currency
      2. Excess demand
2. History of Deficits
   A. Resulting conflicts
   B. Debtor/Creditor nations since World War I
   C. Effects of tariffs
   D. Effects on domestic employment
   E. Effects on U.S. asset ownership
3. Political Effects
   A. Germany—post-Versailles Treaty
   B. Japan—quest for oil
   C. OPEC oil embargo
4. Legislative/Monetary Programs
   A. Role of central banks
   B. Bretton-Woods Accords
   C. Plaza Accords
5. Economic Opinions
   A. Nicholas Brady (U.S. Treasury Secretary)
   B. Alan Greenspan (Dir.. Federal Reserve Board)
   C. Helmut Kohl (West German Chancellor)
6. Implications
   A. Effects on U.S. economy

B. How to reduce problem (options)
   1. Trade barriers
   2. Import taxes
   3. Export restrictions
   4. Favored nation status
C. Employment
D. Creditor nation status
E. Forecasts:
   1. Various scenarios

Note that stack "G" cards should be left out of this outline. They will be incorporated, if at all, as you prepare your first draft.

This outline has been prepared solely by using the 3 x 5 card notes taken at the library. What about your own thoughts, ideas, interpretations, etc.? Assign a number to yourself, just as if you were a library book, and write down your own notes on 3 x 5 cards following the same rules as before. You may do this for a brilliant sentence to start the introduction, an idea you thought up that you think may help in the transition from one topic to the next, or anything else you expect to include in your paper that doesn't appear on one of your library note cards.

Once again, you will see how this system continues to make life easier as you move to the next step—the first draft.

First Draft

You're quick, so you probably won't be surprised if I tell you that a good deal of your first draft is done already. It's all on your note cards!

Let's go back to the cards in stack "A" that are concerned with a definition of the deficit and start putting them in the order you think they should appear in the paper.

For example, one note card might contain a Ronald Reagan quote about the trade deficit, another a basic definition of the word "deficit" from a dictionary, a third a more detailed explanation of specifically what a "trade deficit" is. You may decide to lead off with the quote, follow with the basic definition and lead into the more detailed explanation, then move on to the "Causes" section. Simply put the three cards in the order in which you expect them to appear in your paper.

Now move on to the rest of the cards in stack "A"—all of which should be dealing with one of the two causes you intend to write about—and start putting them in the order in which you think they should appear.

Before you move on, be sure to go through your miscellaneous cards (stack "G") and your own notes to see which of them you may wish to include in this opening section of your paper.

Now, using your orderly cards as your source, write or type the information they contain as a first draft. The better your notes and the skill with which you have organized them, the easier such a first draft will be. Here are some pointers to make any first draft even easier:

• Just get the information down in whatever order you've initially decided upon. Don't worry yet about particular wording, punctuation, sentence structure, spelling, transitions from one idea to the next, neatness or anything else! In other words, if you're a perfectionist, suspend your perfection for this draft.

• When you've completed your draft of the first section of your paper, read through it. Presuming that a sentence here or there will have to be added for transition, does it make sense? Does it flow? Does one thought or fact lead logically to the next? If so, great! If not, try moving some things around until you're happier with it. Cutting and pasting hand- or typewritten copy is the easiest way to do this. Don't worry about appearances—all you're trying to do is get everything down on paper for the first time in a reasonable order. Perfection comes later.

• If you can't get to a point where it all seems to hang together, you may be missing an important fact, idea or inter-pretation—"holes" in your paper that you'll need to fill. Make a list of the information you need to obtain in order to complete your draft.

• Do one section (major heading of your detailed outline) at a time, but if you get hung up on one, move on to the next.

• When you reach the end of the last section, go back to the beginning and reread the entire draft—not for style, but for content. Again, make sure any "holes" are noted so you can get the information to fill them.

Just as the note cards make shuffling and re-shuffling the order of your research very easy, so a word processor or computer makes moving copy around much easier (and clean-er) than cutting and pasting together snippets of paper. If you have either, you'll find reorganizing your papers and going from first to second to final draft much faster and easier. You'll also find most word processing programs now come with built-in dictionaries, so checking your spelling is easier than ever. If you can afford one—and they are still not cheap by any definition—I think you will find some kind of computer will pay off in the long run. If you can't, just get the scissors and glue ready!

Back To The Library

Armed with blank note cards, your bibliographic cards and the list of "holes" you need to fill, go back to the library and find the information you require. Follow all the regular rules for note taking. When you're finished, take these new note cards and incorporate the information they contain into your first draft.

Second Draft

It's time to worry about all of the things I told you not to worry about when you were writing the first draft—sentence structure, transitions, spelling, format, grammar, cliches, and all the rest of the "writing" details.

Using your first draft as a guide, start trying to polish your writing. Remember, with the exception of some English teachers who put a premium on writing skill, few of your teachers or professors will be expecting you to write a non-fiction paper that would rival Tom Wolfe. They want to see a neatly-presented, well-thought-out, logically-written paper that communicates your ideas and verifies the completeness of your research. But they *will* be concerned if spelling, grammar, etc. are woefully poor.

So *don't* spend umpteen hours looking up every other word in your thesaurus so you can write "munificent" rather than "unselfish" or "supplication" rather than "cry."

Do spend those hours making sure that your paper logically flows from one idea to the next and that the points you are trying to make are *clearly* and *concisely* presented.

Keep your sentences uncomplicated—a sentence that becomes a page-long paragraph, no matter how brilliantly crafted, is too long a sentence.

Work at your own speed and in the way you work best. Some people prefer to write out the entire paper, then go back over it again and again, producing three, four, six, or even more drafts, until they get it all right. Personally, I like working on one section at a time, getting it virtually perfect before I move on to the next.

When your draft is at the point that you feel it is complete, stop. Walk away from it for a couple of hours, a day, even longer. Then look it over again and see if it seems as complete after the delay. If not, fix the sections you're not happy with. If it's OK, you're almost done.

A Time For Perfection

Presuming the writing of your paper is now complete, go through, word for word, line by line, and make sure every word is spelled correctly, every comma and period is in place, every quote has quotation marks, every sentence is structured properly.

This is the proofreading stage and it is certainly as important as any other. The best-written paper in the world could get a lower grade simply because too many of those well-written words are misspelled!

It's not a bad idea when you've completed your proofing to pass a copy along to a friend and let him or her read it again. Take it from a writer—it's amazing how many mistakes I miss, no matter how many times I proof a manuscript, simply because I wrote it. Familiarity may not breed contempt, but it does breed contemlt.

The Final Step

It's time to immortalize your final draft—write it on clean white paper, type it, have it typed or run it off your word processor or computer.

Again, make sure you have followed your teacher's formatting instructions—double-spaced, typed vs. written, cover page, whatever.

When the final pristine copy is in your hands, there's only one thing left to do before turning it in on time—proof it one more time...especially if you've had someone else type it. There's nothing worse than turning in a paper from which a typist has inadvertently left out sentences or even whole paragraphs (and I've had it happen!), let alone a series of typos that make all your previous proofing fruitless.

Then turn it in and wait for your "A!"

Oral Reports

There are some key differences between preparing an oral report and writing one, especially if you do not want to make the mistake of just reading a written report in front of the class.

First of all, I would recommend utilizing the same 3 x 5 card system for note taking. Depending on your own skills, you can then go so far as to write your entire paper, perhaps with a little less emphasis on spelling, in order to convince yourself you have the facts and figures in the order you want and can present them in the right words. Alternatively, you can write no draft at all, simply utilizing the note cards as your first draft and, through shuffling them, "write" your paper enough to get it in the shape you need.

However far you feel you need to take your "drafting" stage, once you feel you are ready to actually put your report together, I would take a stack of clean note cards and write down the information you want to refer to during your report in the order in which you plan to cover it.

I've found that trying to shuffle a bunch of papers in front of a class is difficult and that note cards that fit in the palm of your hand are a lot easier to use. But only if the notes on them are very short and to the point, to act as "triggers" rather than verbatim cue cards—hanging on to 300 note cards is as difficult as a a sheaf of papers.

So remember: You'll actually be holding these cards in your sweaty palms and speaking from them, so write notes rather than whole sentences. The shorter the notes—and the more often you practice your report so each note triggers the right detailed information—the more effective your report will be. (And the less you will have to look at them, making eye contact with your class and teacher easier.)

As far as ways to make your oral reports more effective, we've already talked about some in chapter 5, but here are a few more:

• Pick out one person to talk to—preferably a friend, but an animated and/or interested person will do—and direct your talk to them.

• Practice, *practice,* **practice** your presentation. Nerves are often because of a lack of confidence. The more confident you are that you know your material, the less nervous you will be. And the better and more spontaneous will be your presentation.

• If you are like me and suffer from the involuntary "shakes" at the mere thought of standing in front of a roomful of people, make sure you can use a lecturn, desk or something to cling to.

• Take a deep breath before you go to the front of the class. And don't worry about pausing, even taking another deep breath or two, if you lose your place or find your confidence slipping away.

• If every trick in the world still doesn't steady you down, consider taking a public speaking course (Dale Carnegie, *et al*), joining the Toastmasters Club, or seeking out similar extracurricular help.

8

HOW TO

Study
For
Tests

8

Quizzes. Midterms. Finals.

PSAT. ACT. SAT.

GMAT. GRE. LSAT.

Civil Service exams. Aptitude tests. Employment tests.

Throughout your educational life—and, more than likely, the rest of your life as well—testing will be an inevitable if sometimes frightening and distressing reality. So the sooner you master the techniques of preparing for, taking and mastering tests, the better off you will be.

Testing is employed for two primary reasons. The first is to gauge your mastery of a particular subject or material. It thus helps establish the minimum standards of achievement you must attain to move up to the next rung of the ladder—the next grade, next course (acceptance to many college courses is based on your successfully passing another course first), next pay level, next job level.

It's second function is to determine the relative standing of one person to another. This has the desired effect of reducing the number of applicants for a single college slot or limiting a final job interview to those best qualified. And, of course, of giving your teacher a "curve" on which to grade you and your classmates.

What Do They Want To Know?

Before you can decide how to study for a particular test, it's imperative that you know exactly what you're being tested on. Preparing for a weekly quiz is far different than preparing for a final exam. And the biggest final of your life is child's play compared to "monster tests" like the oral exams I faced just before graduating college—which covered everything I was supposed to have learned in four years of attendance! Studying for a standardized test like the SAT, ACT or GRE is also completely different—you can't pull out your textbook and, knowing what chapters are being included, just "bone up."

The structure of the test is also of paramount importance, not necessarily in terms of how you study, but in terms of how you tackle the test once you get your test book.

Remember to keep these two key factors in mind as you go through the specific advice in this chapter and adapt that advice according to the specific circumstances in which you find yourself.

What Are You Afraid Of?

Tests are scary creatures. So before I start meting out test-taking techniques, let's tackle one of the key problems many of you will face—test anxiety, that all-too-common reaction to tests characterized by sweaty palms, a blank mind and the insane urge to flee to Pago Pago on the next available cargo ship.

Take heart—very few people look forward to a test; more of you are afraid of tests than you'd think. But that doesn't mean you *have* to fear them.

Since we all recognize the competitive nature of tests, being in the right frame of mind when taking them is important. Some of us rise to the occasion when facing such a challenge. Others are thrown off balance by the pressure. Both reactions probably have little to do with one's level of knowledge, relative intelligence or amount of preparation. The smartest kids in your class may be the ones most afraid of tests.

Generally speaking, the best way to avoid the pitfalls of the extraordinary pressures of a testing situation is to place yourself in that environment as often as possible. Yep. Practice helps.

But there are some other, surprisingly simple things you can do to give yourself an edge by being less *on* edge.

Handling Anxiety

Few people enter a testing site cool, calm and ready for action. Most of us have various butterflies gamboling in our stomachs, sweat glands operating in overdrive and a sincere desire to be somewhere else...anywhere else.

Even if you're just entering high school, you have a few years of tests under your belt and should have some idea of how well or poorly you react to a testing situation. If the answer is "not well," start trying some of the following options until you find the one(s) that work for you.

"I Know I Can, I Know I Can"

The more pressure you put on yourself—the larger you allow a test (and, of course, your hoped-for good scores) to loom in your own mind—the less you are helping yourself. And, of course, the bigger the test really *is,* the more likely you are to keep reminding yourself of its importance.

No matter how important a test really may be to your career—and your scores on some *can* have a major effect on where you go to college, whether you go on to graduate school, whether you get the job you want—it is just as important to *de*-emphasize that test's importance in your mind. This should have no effect on your preparation—study like your life depended on it!—just the relative importance you place on the test in your mind.

Keeping the whole experience in perspective might also help: Twenty years from now, nobody will remember, or care, what you scored on any test...no matter how life-threatening or life-determining you feel that test is right now.

And don't underestimate that old standby, positive thinking: Thoughts *can* become self-fulfilling prophecies. Tell yourself often enough "be careful, you're fall over that step," and you just might. Tell yourself often enough "I'm going to fail this test" and you just might. Likewise, keep convincing yourself that you are as prepared as anyone and are going to "ace" the sucker, and you are already ahead of the game.

A Little Traveling Music, Sam

You've already found that scheduling breaks during your study routine makes it easier for you to focus on your books and complete your assignments faster and with more concentration. Scheduling breaks during tests has the same effects.

During a one-hour test, you may have no time to go out for a stroll. But during a two- or three-hour final, a major test like the SAT, etc., there's no reason not to schedule one, two or even more breaks on a periodic basis...or whenever you feel you need them most. Such time-outs can consist of a bathroom stop, a quick walk up and down the hall, or just a minute of relaxation in your seat before you continue the test.

No matter what the time limits or pressures, don't feel you cannot afford such a brief respite. You may need it *most* when you're convinced you can *least* afford it.

I'm Relaxing As Fast As I Can!

If your mind is a jumble of facts and figures, names and dates, you may find it difficult to zero in on the specific details you need to recall, even if you know all the material backwards and forwards. The adrenaline rushing through your system may just make "instant retrieval" impossible.

The simplest relaxation technique is deep breathing. Just lean back in your chair, relax your muscles and take three very deep breaths (count to ten while you hold each one). For many of you, that's the only relaxing technique you'll ever need.

There are a variety of meditation techniques which may also work for you. Each is based on a similar principle—focusing your mind on one thing to the exclusion of everything else. While you're concentrating on the object of your meditation (even if the object is nothing, a nonsense word or a spot on the wall), your mind can't be thinking about anything else, which allows it to slow down a bit. The next time you can't focus, try sitting back, taking three deep breaths and concentrating for a minute or two on the word "Mu." I think you'll find when you're done that you are in a far more relaxed state and ready to tackle any test.

If you feel you need such help, consider learning some sort of meditation technique, whether Silva mind control, transcendental meditation, or even self-hypnosis.

Ah, hypnosis. Another alternative. While I question its effectiveness as a study method—I'm not sure if learning self-hypnosis can help you read faster, remember more, etc.—it can be an excellent relaxation technique, as it is really just a form of meditation.

Whatever such technique you feel you need to use, remember an important fact: The more you believe in the technique, the more it will work. Just like your belief that you're going to "ace" that test!

Something In Common

Some rites of preparation are pertinent to any test, from a weekly quiz to the SAT and everything in between:

Plan Ahead

I'll admit it. When I was a student, even in college, my attention span tended to be bounded by the weekends. Tell me in October that there would be a big test the first week of December and I'd remember, probably, around November 31st.

Of such habits are cramming, crib sheets and failing marks made.

The key to avoiding all of these unpleasantries is review. But *regular, periodic review*. The more often you review, the less often you will have to pull all-nighters the week of the test.

You already will have stayed on top of the material, written down and asked questions that arose from your reviews and gone over class and textbook notes to make sure you understand everything. Your last-minute review will be relatively leisurely and organized, not feverish and harried.

In chapter 4, I included a review schedule on our Project Board (see pages 90 & 91). My suggestion is to set up the simplest review schedule possible, but one you will stick to. For example, you might simply review one subject a week until you have reviewed the previous work for each subject. Then start over again. Sunday mornings might be set aside for this process. Or a weeknight that you normally have free.

Alternatively, you can review the previous week's work in *all* subjects *every* week. Some of you may prefer this method; I personally find it a little unwieldy, preferring to concentrate on just one subject and being able to work as long as necessary without worrying about having to "move on."

Later in this chapter I will be talking about the possibility of forming a study group, which might make the review process even easier.

Get Me To The Church

Doing poorly on a test is discouraging. Doing poorly on a test you felt ready for is depressing. Missing the test entirely is devastating.

It's imperative that you know when and where all tests are scheduled and allow ample time to get to them.

If you're still in high school, getting to a particular test shouldn't be too hard—it will probably be held during your regular class period and in your normal classroom.

But in college, tests may be scheduled at hours different than the normal class period and at an entirely different site.

Likewise, major out-of-school tests like the SAT may not even be held at your school. In such cases, make sure you allow enough time to drive, or be driven, to wherever you have to be...especially if no one is quite sure how to get there!

As soon as you know the time and location of any major test—midterm, final, SAT, etc.—enter them on your weekly calendar. Whether in high school, college or grad school, most schools set aside a week, two or even more for final exams. This "exam period" is usually clearly marked in your college handbook, announced in class (usually on the first day), printed on your class syllabus, etc.

Sometimes, in addition to your regular reading and assignments, the teacher will assign "optional" reading at the beginning of a course. These books, articles, etc. may never be discussed in any class...but material from them may well be included on a test, especially a final exam. If you have neglected to add this supplementary reading to your regular weekly assignments calendar, but wish to read it before the test, make sure you allow enough time to buy or find these books. A lot of other students may have also left such reading to the last minute and you may be unable to find the material you need if you wait too long.

Lastly, bring whatever materials you need to the test, from pens and pencils to calculators. I also recommend— especially for a long test like the SAT—that you bring along a candy bar, lifesavers, or some other "quick energy" snack to help buck you up when you need to give yourself a figurative "slap in the face."

Although many testing booklets will include room for notes, it may not be sufficient for your purposes. If you are asked to write three, five or even more essay questions, you will want a lot of scratch paper to outline and organize your thoughts before you put pen to paper. Likewise, a particularly complex math test may quickly use up every margin on the test. So bring along a separate writing tablet or even a stack of scrap paper. There are few situations in which their use won't be allowed.

If You Didn't Listen Before

Review, review, review. If you don't follow my advice for periodic review, you must be sure, especially for midterms and finals, to set aside enough time to do all the review and studying you need in the week or two before the test.

The more material you need to review, the more important it is to clear your schedule. A four-, five- or six-course load covering twenty, forty or more books, lectures and discussions, papers and projects, easily generates hundreds of pages of notes. Reviewing them, understanding them, studying them will require your full-time effort for a week, even two. So make sure all other end-of-term work, especially major projects like papers, are out of the way.

Whether you need to schedule a solid two weeks for a complete review or just two or three days because you have already reviewed most of your course work on a regular basis, make sure you schedule the time you've allocated on your weekly calendar, allowing more time for the subjects in which you are weakest, of course.

Test Yourself

Yes, there are teachers who test you on the most mundane details from every book assigned, requiring you to review every book, every note, every scribble.

I don't think most teachers work that way.

The areas on which your teacher seems to place his or her emphasis—according to time spent in class, questions asked on quizzes, midterms, etc.—should be the same areas you concentrate on for a major test. (Which is why you should try to save copies of every test you are given. They are excellent study aids!)

In general, take the time to eliminate from consideration, with the possible exception of a cursory review, material you are convinced is not important enough to be included on an upcoming test. This will automatically give you more time to concentrate on those areas you are sure *will* be included on the test.

Just as you have made it a habit to write down questions as you study your texts, why not try to construct your own tests? And remember: the harder you make them, the better prepared and more confident you will be walking into the test.

What Are Friends For?

Surprisingly enough, I was 35 and a devoted watcher of the television show *The Paper Chase* before I was introduced to the concept of a study group. Now this series was supposed to be about a Law School that seemed just this side of hell, so sharing the load with other students wasn't just a good idea— it was virtually mandatory to survive. If I had thought of the idea myself, even while I was in high school, I would have probably started one. And I was a good student.

The idea is simple: Find a small group of like-minded students—four to six seems to be an optimum number—and share notes, question each other, prepare for tests together. To be effective, obviously, the students you pick to be in your group should share all, or at least most, of your classes.

Search out students who are smarter than you, but not *too* much smarter than you. If they are on a level far beyond your own, you'll soon be left in the dust and be more discouraged than ever. On the other hand, if you choose students who are too far beneath your level, you'll enjoy the spotlight of being the "Brain" but be missing the point of the group—the challenge of other minds to spur you on.

Study groups can be organized in a variety of ways. Each member could be assigned primary responsibility for a single class, including preparing detailed notes from lectures and discussion groups. If supplementary reading is recommended but not required, that person could be responsible for doing all such reading and preparing detailed summaries. (The extra work you will thus have to do in one class will be offset by the extra work others will be doing for you.)

Alternatively, everybody can be responsible for his or her own notes, but the group could act as an ad hoc discussion group, refining your understanding of key points, working on problems together, questioning each other, practicing for tests, etc.

Even if you find only one or two other students willing to work with you, I think such cooperation would be invaluable, especially in preparing for major exams.

Four Hundred Twenty Questions!?

Is it wrong to ask the teacher what kind of test to expect? Absolutely not. Will he or she always tell you? Absolutely not.

But it is also not wrong to research that teacher's tests from previous years—students a year or two ahead of you can sometimes be invaluable help in this effort.

Why? Because, like most of us, teachers are creatures of habit. While you certainly shouldn't expect to find questions

173

that will be duplicated, you can glean a few key things from previous tests, like the format the teacher seems to prefer and the areas that seem to be stressed. Don't take any of this as a "given," however; even creatures of the most set habits have been known to turn over a new leaf now and then.

The Day Of The Test

If the test is not simply during a regular class period, make sure to arrive at the test site early. Based on your preferences (from chapter 2), sit where you like. Be careful, however. There may be some variations here you have to take into account. In a test where there are 200 or 300 people in a room, there is a distinct advantage to sitting near the front. You can hear instructions and the answers to questions better. And you generally get the test first. And if you normally prefer sitting near a window, but there is construction outside, you would, one expects, change your preference for that day.

Know The Ground Rules

Will you be penalized for guessing? The teacher, for example, may inform you that he will add two points for every correct answer but *subtract* one point for every incorrect one. This will certainly effect whether you guess or not...or, at the very least, how many potential answers you feel you need to eliminate before the odds of guessing are in your favor.

Are the questions or sections weighted? Some tests may have two, three or more sections, some of which count for very little—10%, 20% of your final score—while one, usually a major essay, may be more heavily weighted—50% or more of your grade. This should drastically alter the time you spend on each section.

Answer Every Fourth Question

Read and understand the directions. As I stressed in chapter 7, you could seemingly do everything right, but not follow your teacher's explicit directions, in which case everything's wrong. If you're supposed to check off *every* correct answer to each question in a multiple choice test—and you're assuming only one is correct—you're going to miss a lot of answers! If you're to pick one essay question out of three, or two out of five, that's a lot different than trying to answer every one. You won't do it. And even if you do, the teacher will probably only grade the first two. Because you needed to allocate enough time to do the other three, it's highly doubtful your first two answers will be so detailed and perfect that they will be able to stand alone.

And be aware of time. Again, if questions or sections are weighted, you will want to make sure you allow extra time for those that count the most. Better to do a superior job on the two sections that count for 90% of the score and whip through the 10% section as the teacher is collecting booklets than get every one of the 10% questions right and barely get started on the essay question that counts for 50%!

I know students who, before they write one answer, look through the entire test and break it down into time segments—allocating 20 minutes for section one, 40 for section two, etc. Even on multiple choice tests—they count the total number of questions, divide by the time allotted and set "goals" on what time they should reach question 10, question 25, 50, etc.

I never did it. But I think it's a great idea...if it turns out to be a workable organizational tool for you and not just one more layer of pressure.

Test Taking Strategies

Presuming you know the answers to the various questions raised above, what techniques can you use to better your test scores?

Pick And Choose

There are three ways to attack a test:

1. Start at the first question and keep going, question by question, until you reach the end, never leaving a question until you have either answered it fully or, if multiple choice, made an educated guess.

2. Answer every easy question—the ones you know the answers to without any thinking at all or those requiring the simplest calculations—first, then go back and do the harder ones.

3. Answer the hardest questions first, then go back and do the easy ones.

None of these three options is inherently right or wrong. Each may work for different individuals. (And I'm assuming that these three approaches are all in the context of the test format. Weighted sections may well affect your strategy.)

The first approach is, in one sense, the quickest, in that no time is wasted reading through the whole test trying to pick out either the easiest or hardest questions. Presuming that you do not allow yourself to get stumped by a single question so that you spend an inordinate amount of time on it, it is probably the method most of you should employ (and already do). Remember, though, to leave questions that confuse you from the outset to the end and allocate enough time to both go back to those you haven't answered and check *all* your answers thoroughly.

The second approach ensures that you will maximize your right answers—you're putting those you are certain of down first. It may also, presuming that you knock off these easy ones relatively fast, give you the most time to work on those that you find particularly vexing.

The last approach is actually the one I use. In fact, I make it a point to do the very hardest question first, then work my way "down" the difficulty ladder. It may sound like a strange strategy to you, but let me explain the psychology. First of all, I figure if time pressure starts getting to me at the end of the test, I would rather be in a position to answer the easiest questions—and a lot of them—in the limited time left than ones I really have to think about. After all, by the end of the test, my mind won't be working as well as at the beginning!

And that's a major benefit of the third approach: When I am most "up," most awake, most alert, I am tackling those questions that require the most analysis, thinking, interpretation, etc. When I am most tired—near the end—I am answering the questions that are virtually "gimmes."

At the same time, I am also giving myself a real shot of confidence. As soon as I finish the first hard question, I already feel better. When I finish all of the hard ones, everything is down hill.

It is not the approach for everybody, but it may be for you.

I would always, however, try to ensure adequate time to at least put down an answer for every question. Better to get one question wrong and complete three other answers than get one right and leave three blanks. And don't fall into the "answer daze," that blank stare some students get when they just can't think of an answer...for ten minutes. Do *something*. Better to move on and get that one question wrong than waste invaluable time doing nothing.

Discriminate And Eliminate

There is usually nothing wrong with guessing, unless, of course, you know wrong answers will be penalized. Even then, as I've pointed out, guessing is not necessarily wrong. The question is how *much* to guess.

If there is no penalty for wrong answers, you should *never* leave an answer blank. But you should also do everything you can to decrease the odds against you. If every multiple choice question gives you four possible answers, you have a 25% chance of being right (and, of course, a 75% chance of being wrong) each time you have to guess.

But if you can eliminate a single answer—one you are reasonably certain cannot be right—odds are your "guess" will be right 33% (and wrong only 67% of the time).

And, of course, if you can get down to a choice between two answers, it's just like flipping a coin: 50-50. In the long run, you will guess as many right as wrong.

Even if there is a penalty for guessing, I would probably pick one answer if I had managed to increase my chances of getting the right one to 50-50.

I Could Write A Book

Approach essay questions the same way you would a paper. While you can't check your textbook or go to the library to do research, the facts, ideas, comparisons, etc. you need are in your own cerebral library—your mind.

Step One: On a blank sheet of paper, write down all the facts, ideas, concepts, etc. you feel should be included in your answer.

Step Two: Organize them in the order in which they should appear. You don't have to rewrite your notes into a detailed outline—why not just number each note according to where you want to place it?

Step Three: Compose your first paragraph, working on it just as long and as hard as I suggested you do on your papers. It should summarize and introduce the key points you will make in your essay. ***This is where superior essay answers are made or broken.***

Step Four: Write your essay.

Step Five: Reread your essay and, if necessary, add points left out, correct spelling, grammar, etc.

If there is a particular fact you know is important and should be included but you just don't remember it, guess if you can. Otherwise, just leave it out and do the best you can. If the rest of your essay is well-thought-out and organized and clearly communicates all the other points that should be included, I doubt most teachers will mark you down too severely for such an omission.

Remember: Few teachers will be impressed by length. A well-organized, well-constructed, specific answer to their question will always get you a better grade than "shotgunning"— writing down everything you know in the faint hope that you will actually hit something.

If you don't have the faintest clue what the question means, ask. If you still don't have any idea of the answer—and I mean *zilch*—leave it blank. Writing down everything you think you know about the supposed subject in the hopes that one or two things will actually have something to do with the question is, in my mind, a waste of everyone's time. Better you allocate the time you would waste to other portions of the test and do a better job on those.

First Out Could Be First Failed

Leave time at the end of every test to recheck your answers. And speaking of time, don't make a habit of leaving tests early. There is little to be gained from supposedly "impressing" the teacher and other students with how smart you (think you) are by being first to finish. Take the time to make sure you've done your best. If you are completely satisfied with your answers to all questions, it's fine to leave, even if you are first. But in general, slowing down will help you avoid careless mistakes. Speed kills.

Likewise, don't worry about what everybody else is doing. Even if you're the last person left, who cares? Everybody else could have failed, no matter how early and confidently they strode from the room! So take all the time you need and do the best you can.

Open Book Tests

Answer the questions you don't need the book for first, including those where you're fairly sure and know where to check the answers in your book. Star these latter ones.

Then use the book. Check your starred answers first and erase the stars once you have checked. Then work on those questions on which you must rely fully on the book.

Standardized Tests

The various standardized tests used in college and graduate school admissions—SAT, ACT, LSAT, GRE, etc.—require their own pointers. These, like my oral exams at the end of four years of college, are not specific to any one course or even one grade. Rather, they are attempting to assess your ability to apply mathematical concepts, read and understand various passages and demonstrate word skills.

Despite their ephemeral nature, you *can* study for them by practicing. There are a variety of companies specializing in preparing students for each of these tests—your school might even sponsor its own course. And any bookstore will probably have shelves of preparation guides.

Given their importance, I would recommend investing the time and money in any such reputable course—Stanley Kaplan, Princeton Review, BAR/BRI, etc.—or, at the very least, buying one of the major preparation books. Since these are, indeed, *standard*ized tests, learning and utilizing specific techniques pertinent to them and practicing on tests given previously can significantly increase your scores, if only because you will feel less anxious and have a better idea of what's in store for you.

If you are an avid reader and understand what you read, do well in school in most subjects, but especially English and Math, and "test well," you may not feel you need such remedial help. That's OK, too. But do note that many of the questions on these tests are word-related—SWAN is to DUCK as YOGURT is to ...—testing both your basic vocabulary and your specific understanding of synonyms (words with similar meanings) and antonyms (words with opposite meanings). So if you don't decide to take one of the review courses, you might still consider getting a good vocabulary book—*Increase Your Word Power in 30 Days* or something similar—as a study aid for such tests.

There are students who achieve exceptional test scores on their SATs and go on to compile barely adequate college records. These people are said to "test well." The testing environment doesn't throw them and they have sufficient prior experience to have a decided edge on the rest of the competition. Others "choke" during such tests but wind up at the top of the career pyramid.

So such testing must be kept in perspective. Though one method of predicting success, such tests are not, by any means, perfect oracles. Nor are their conclusions inalienable. Many people have succeeded in life without ever doing particularly well on achievement tests.

Remember: Testing is a skill which can, to a great extent, be learned. Since it is already a part of your life and always will be, you'd be wise to take the time *now* to master the fundamentals of smart test taking. Just reading this chapter has probably helped immensely, even if all it did for you was remove some of the mystery from the testing process.

Answers To Exercises

Chapter 1

1) T 2) F 3) T 4) T 5) F 6) T 7) T 8) F 9) F 10) F

Chapter 3

Reading Comprehension

Fiction: 1) C 2) C 3) D. History: 1) B 2) A 3) A 4) A. Current Events: 1) D 2) A 3) D 4) B 5) B

Test Your Literary I. Q

1) If you're in high school, give yourself 3 points for each you're familiar with; if in college or beyond, give yourself 2 points.

2) High school: 7 points for each; College and up: 3 points.

3) Everyone: 2 points for each author read

4) Everyone: 2 points for each book read

5) High school: 2 points for each correct answer; College and up: 1 point

183

Answers to Question 5)

1) Eugene O'Neill
2) George Orwell
3) James Joyce
4) Henry Fielding
5) Tennessee Williams
6) Thomas Wolfe
7) Aesop!
8) Lewis Carroll
9) Erich Maria Remarque
10) Theodore Dreiser
11) Sinclair Lewis
12) Geoffrey Chaucer
13) Sinclair Lewis
14) Sylvia Plath
15) Aldous Huxley
16) Fyodor Dostoevsky
17) Joseph Heller
18) Marcel Proust
19) John Steinbeck
20) George Bernard Shaw
21) Arthur Miller
22) James Fenimore Cooper
23) F. Scott Fitzgerald
24) Joseph Conrad
25) Miguel de Cervantes
26) Washington Irving
27) Emily Bronte
28) Edith Wharton
29) Thomas Hardy
30) Ernest Hemingway
31) Jonathan Swift
32) William Shakespeare
33) Mark Twain
34) Homer
35) Rudyard Kipling
36) Hemingway
37) Walt Whitman
38) Victor Hugo
39) Shakespeare
40) Sinclair Lewis
41) Shakespeare
42) Herman Melville
43) Richard Wright
44) George Orwell
45) W. Somerset Maugham
46) John Steinbeck
47) Charles Dickens
48) Dickens
49) Ken Kesey
50) Shakespeare
51) Thornton Wilder
52) Leo Tolstoy
53) John Milton
54) Dostoevsky
55) Robert Louis Stevenson
56) Nathaniel Hawthorne
57) Hermann Hesse
58) Thomas Mann
59) George Eliot
60) D. H. Lawrence
61) Hermann Hesse
62) Hesse
63) F. Scott Fitzgerald
64) Jane Austen
65) J. D. Salinger
66) Tom Wolfe
67) Alexandre Dumas
68) Dostoevsky
69) Madison, Hamilton & Jay

70) Hemingway
71) Isaac Asimov
72) James Jones
73) Pearl Buck
74) Robert Frost
75) Sir Arthur Conan Doyle
76) Dickens
77) Dostoevsky
78) Shakespeare
79) H. G. Wells
80) Charlotte Bronte
81) J. R. R. Tolkien
82) Kahlil Gibran
83) Edgar Allan Poe
84) Bertolt Brecht
85) Stephen Crane
86) Thomas Hardy

87) Hemingway
88) Dickens
89) H. G. Wells
90) Vergil
91) T. S. Eliot
92) Franz Kafka
93) Mark Twain
94) Shakespeare
95) James Joyce
96) George Bernard Shaw
97) William Thackery
98) Henry David Thoreau
99) Joseph Conrad
100) Shakespeare

Your Literary I. Q

High School	Rating	College
0—100	Poor	0—250
100—149	Satisfactory	251—350
150—200	Average	351—450
201—300	Above Average	451—550
300—350	Very Good	551—650
350—400	Superior	651—750
Over 400	Outstanding	Over 750

Chapter 6

1) B 2) A, B &/or C (I didn't claim there was only one right answer!) 3) B 4) C 5) B 6) C 7) A & B 8) C 9) A

Index

❑ **High Impact Resumes and Letters**, 3rd Edition, by Krannich and Banis. ISBN 0-942710-20-7. Paper. 8 1/2 x 11. 180 pages. $13.95

❑ **Intervie** 2710-
19-3, Pa aid.

❑ **The Com** yl
Krannich tpaid.

❑ **Public S**
Harrison paid.

❑ **Interna** SBN
0-913589

❑ **After Co**
ISBN 0-9

❑ **Parentin**
Sally Val
postpaid

❑ **What's N**
0-913589

❑ **The Com**
Faustin
$11.95   postp

TO ORDER A
SIMPLY CAL
VISA.